The Etchings of Rembrandt

Also from Westphalia Press
westphaliapress.org

The Etchings of Rembrandt

A Study and History

by P. G. Hamerton

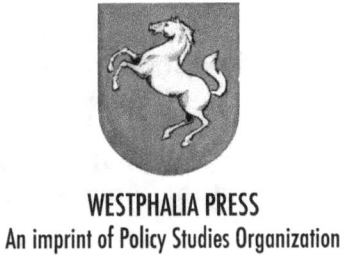

WESTPHALIA PRESS
An imprint of Policy Studies Organization

Westphalia Press
An imprint of Policy Studies Organization
1527 New Hampshire Ave., NW
Washington, D.C. 20036
info@ipsonet.org

ISBN-13: 978-1-63391-589-3
ISBN-10: 1-63391-589-1

Cover design by Jeffrey Barnes:
jbarnes.design

Daniel Gutierrez-Sandoval, Executive Director
PSO and Westphalia Press

Updated material and comments on this edition
can be found at the Westphalia Press website:
www.westphaliapress.org

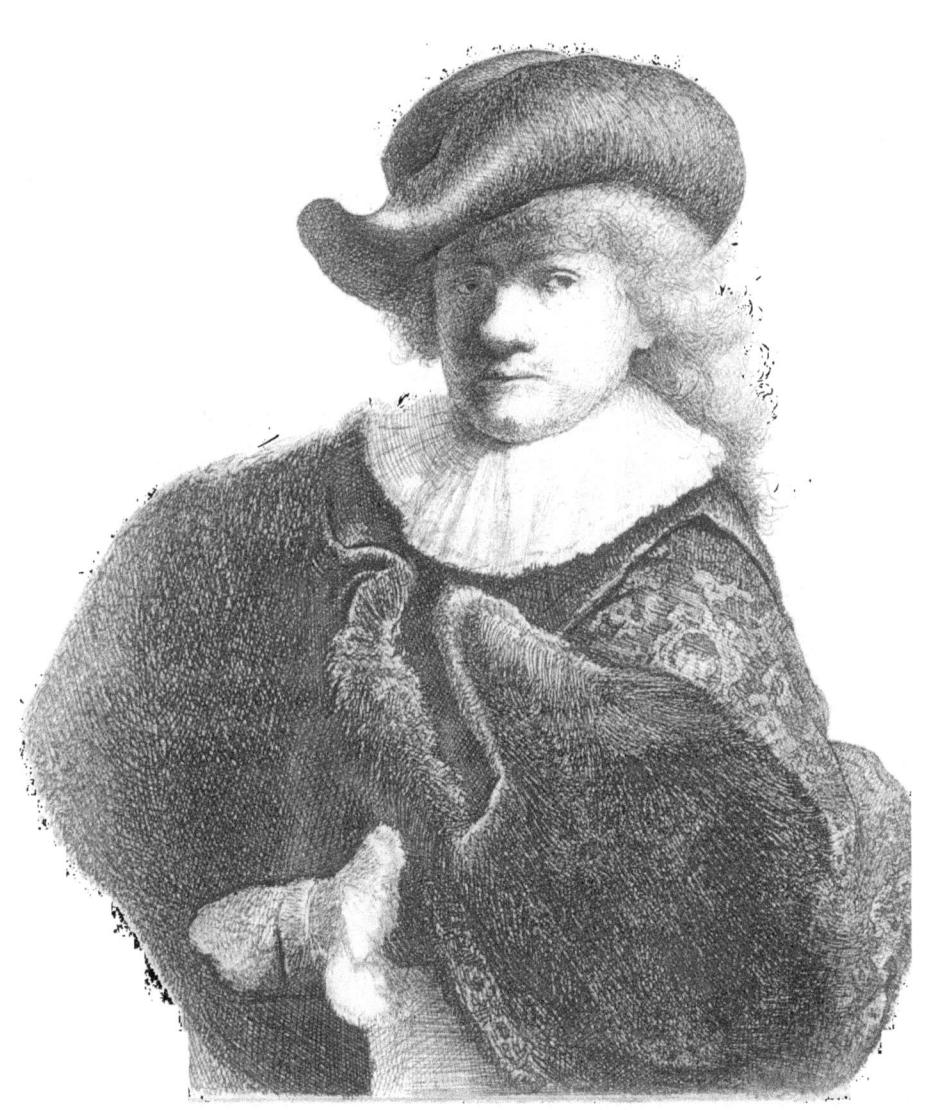

THE DATE OF REMBRANDT'S BIRTH

The date 1607 is according to Vosmaer. Other writers have given 1606, and this has been accepted by Mr. Haden and M. Michel. I had not space to enter into the controversy, and merely trusted the Dutch biographer.

THE ETCHINGS OF REMBRANDT

By

P. G. HAMERTON

Author of "Etching & Etchers," &c.

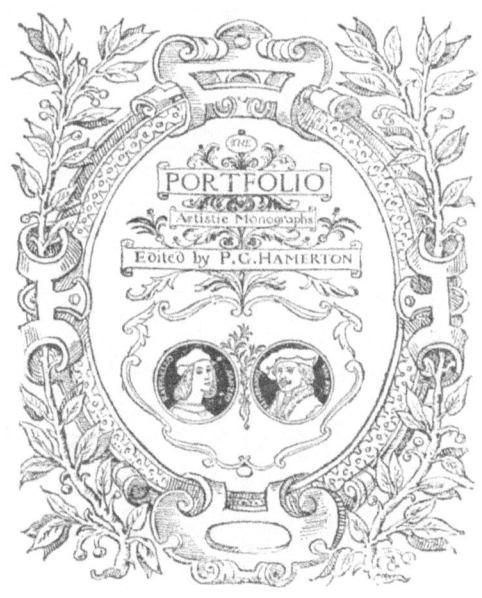

LONDON

SEELEY AND CO. LIMITED, GREAT RUSSELL STREET

NEW YORK: THE MACMILLAN COMPANY

1902

LIST OF ILLUSTRATIONS

PLATES ETCHED IN FACSIMILE BY AMAND DURAND.

ILLUSTRATIONS IN THE TEXT.

THE
ETCHINGS OF REMBRANDT

PART I

THE PLATES CONSIDERED WITH REFERENCE TO THE ARTIST'S BIOGRAPHY

I

THIS little treatise is intended to be an introduction to the study of the etched work of Rembrandt. The notice of him in *Etching and Etchers* was of necessity no more than a short account of what he had done, with a special mention of a few representative plates ; the catalogues of Bartsch, Claussin, Wilson, Charles Blanc, Middleton, and Dutuit, are too voluminous and important to be convenient as handbooks, besides being too mechanical in arrangement for consecutive reading. A memorable exhibition of Rembrandt's etchings was held at the Burlington Fine Arts Club in the year 1877, and the catalogue of it is well known, for two special reasons, to all serious students of Rembrandt, both in England and on the Continent. The first of these reasons is the adoption, at that time unprecedented, of the chronological order in preference to the old classification by subject, and the second is the Introduction by Mr. Seymour Haden, in which he expressed his disbelief in the authenticity of certain famous plates that had been admitted into all previous catalogues. Mr. Haden's argument is of such importance that no subsequent writer can afford to pass it in silence, but it is fully intelligible, in all its bearings, only by advanced students. Besides this, the catalogue in which it appeared was privately printed for the Club, and is not generally accessible. The same objection, so far as ordinary English readers are concerned, applies even to some of the published contributions to Rembrandt literature, which are costly, and printed in foreign languages. For example, the French catalogue by Dutuit, with heliographic reproductions by Charreyre, is sold at six hundred francs. It has therefore seemed to us that there was room for a handbook to the etchings of Rembrandt, published at a low price, and containing a synoptic account arranged in a readable form, and in such a manner that any one who perused it might find himself, with little effort, so far acquainted with the subject that no part of Rembrandt's great performance as an etcher would seem absolutely strange to him.

The systematic study of the works of a great etcher is seldom undertaken by lovers of art who are not led to it by the requirements of a critic or a collector, and yet this systematic study, though it may seem tedious to the amateur, and pedantic to the artist, and though it may be regarded with the most complete indifference by the public generally, has its own rewards to offer in the additional clearness which it imparts to the whole subject, and in the enhanced interest that every separate etching gains from being known in connection with the rest. This kind of study would be impossible for us without the help of the minutely detailed information that the zealous industry of catalogue-makers has accumulated for our use. We are, indeed, infinitely their debtors, for without their labours of love, extending, in some cases, over many years, and rewarded only by the appreciation of the few who know all that such toil involves, the student could never gain a comprehensive view of the total production of a great artist. Even if he had access to a complete collection, it would be impossible for him to know that it was complete.

I have just alluded to two methods in the arrangement of a catalogue, the chronological order and classification by subject. Even in a brief treatise like the present some definite system is necessary, and I have decided to adopt three systems, each for one part of my essay, which will keep them as distinct from each other as possible, both for the reader's convenience and my own. The first is chronological so as to connect the etchings, or many of them, with the inspiring and affecting story of Rembrandt's courageous and troubled existence. One of the great artist's biographers, M. Emile Michel, says that Rembrandt has himself almost invariably enlightened us as to the date of his works, but this, with regard at least to the etchings, is certainly saying too much and therefore it is impossible for me to follow the chronological method exclusively. M. Dutuit, on the other hand, observes that nearly two-thirds of Rembrandt's etchings are without date. This statement is, however, a very great exaggeration of their still too frequent datelessness. Mr. Middleton, in his catalogue, admits three hundred and twenty-nine plates as genuine. Out of these, one hundred and eighty-one are dated, so that the dated plates are in the majority and sufficiently abundant to afford in themselves all that is needed for reference in the first, or biographical, portion of this essay, especially considering that the author, having a limited space at his command, is not under any obligation to refer to everything that Rembrandt executed. Those who try to make complete chronological catalogues are sorely tempted to assign dates that must in many instances be purely, if not wildly, conjectural. Each instance would require to be supported by a separate argument which is seldom given, so that the reader sees that the date is assumed but does not often know why it is assumed. The compiler has, no doubt, gone through a process of reasoning that is satisfactory to himself and might be so to his readers if their faith were not disturbed by other equally authorised compilers. Our teachers do, indeed, arrive at the most divergent and contradictory conclusions. The differences between Vosmaer and Middleton are extremely frequent, and in several instances so wide that it would seem as if there were nothing in the changing manner of Rembrandt's workmanship, or in his tastes and interests so far as the choice of subject is concerned, to justify one in fixing a date within a year or two, or even a decade. For example there is the well-known plate of *The Triumph of Mordecai* to which Vosmaer assigns 1640 or from that to 1645, whereas Middleton fixes 1651. *The Adoration of the Shepherds* was etched, according to Vosmaer, between 1632 and 1640, according to Middleton in 1652. *The Star of the Kings* is dated by Vosmaer 1641, but Middleton puts it twelve years later. When we are assured by the Dutch authority that the date of *The Blind Man seen from behind* is 1651 the English connoisseur throws us back no less than twenty-one years, a little more than one-third of Rembrandt's whole existence. There is, however, one page in Vosmaer's great work which deserves our unqualified approval. It is that in which he gives a list of twenty-one plates for which he declines to fix any date whatever. Writers for whom the fixing of dates is an absolutely over-mastering passion may always safely assume that an etching by Rembrandt was produced between 1607, when the artist came into the world, and 1669, when he went out of it. No other plan is absolutely safe. It might seem possible, at first sight, to assume that Rembrandt took up the etching-needle in 1628, which is the first date we have, and laid it down in 1661, as that is the last, but we have not the slightest proof that he did not begin to etch when he was sixteen instead of twenty-one, or that he did not continue the practice of the art after having, from negligence or discouragement, entirely ceased to put dates upon his productions. The matter may seem to be of slight importance in comparison with the authenticity or the technical excellence of the plates themselves, but it is really more important than, at first sight, it may appear. If we knew exactly the order in which all the plates were executed we might observe with the keenest interest the signs of mental and technical progress. This is possible, in some degree, even with the dated works that are accessible to us, although, as we have seen, they are not very much more than half of the magnificent *Œuvre*.

My rule to refer in the biographical part to dated plates only is a restriction on the side of safety, but there is another equally important, and that is that a critic ought not to refer, except by way of caution, to any plate of whose authenticity he is not perfectly satisfied. The reader not yet familiar with the controversy concerning Rembrandt's etchings may be briefly told in this place that a plate may be signed with his name, and dated, without being necessarily his handiwork. The etchings accumulated in collections under the name of Rembrandt may be classed in these five categories.

1. Those plates of which the conception and execution are equally and entirely those of Rembrandt himself. This category includes both successful plates and failures which are rather numerous in proportion, but the failure is in most instances purely technical and does not greatly interfere with the mental qualities of the performance.

2. Plates of which the idea and design belong to Rembrandt but of which the execution has been partially entrusted to assistants.

3. Plates designed by Rembrandt but executed entirely by others.

4. Plates of which the manual execution is more or less completely due to Rembrandt, but in composing which he made use of borrowed ideas.

5. Plates with which Rembrandt had nothing whatever to do, either mentally or manually.

Now of these five categories, I intend to confine myself, in the two earlier parts of the present essay, entirely to the first. In my third part, I shall enter upon the stony and thorny ground of controversy and deal with the doubtful or contested plates, not that I have any particular eagerness for controversial warfare, but because, in this case it is impossible to keep out of it. Besides, no reasonable person could fall into the illogical fallacy of interpreting an attack upon the authenticity of more or less spurious Rembrandts as an attack upon Rembrandt himself. The truth is that no kinder service can be rendered to a great artist by the most faithful of his admirers than the detection of those works that the cupidity of some, and the uncritical confidence of others, have falsely attributed to him. Every work justly discarded relieves his reputation of a burden, and when we reflect how ready posterity always is to attribute works to celebrities whose names are familiar to it, and how strongly persons who have them in their possession, or desire to sell them, are biassed in favour of such attribution, it seems inevitable that these burdens should be laid upon the memory of the dead.

The absence of concord amongst authorities is shown in the following little table :—

Bartsch (1797) . . . . admits 375 plates.
Claussin (1824) . . . . ,, 365 ,,
Wilson (1836) . . . . ,, 369 ,,
Charles Blanc (1859–61) . . . . ,, 353 ,,
Vosmaer (1868–77) . . . . ,, 353 ,,
Middleton (1878) . . . . 329 ,,
Dutuit (1883) . . . . ,, 363 ,,

Charles Blanc gives a list of twenty-nine rejected plates and makes an addition of seven to the catalogue. Vosmaer accepts the number given by Blanc as well as his system of order. Mr. Middleton gives a list of eighteen rejected studies and sketches with thirty rejected landscapes, and M. Dutuit adds to his catalogue a list of six etchings "attributed to" Rembrandt, and two "falsely attributed." It is unnecessary to go further into these questions at present. The reader sees the necessity for great caution, but I may add, to reassure him, that the great majority of the plates still attributed to Rembrandt bear so visibly the impress of his hand and genius that they are accepted without hesitation by every one who is familiar with his styles (for he had several styles) and with the very different moods of his versatile and generally quite original mind. He sometimes borrowed from others, but not often, and though it is now evident that he accepted assistance in the execution of certain plates that bear his name, we must still remember that he was one of the most personally industrious of great artists and one of those who have been most rarely dependent upon auxiliaries.

It remains only to be added that references to plates will be accompanied, at least once, by the numbers given respectively in the catalogues of Bartsch and Middleton. That of Bartsch, though nearly a hundred years old, is still a living work, in continual requisition, whilst Mr. Middleton's catalogue has the advantages of being written in English eighty years later, and of being easily accessible to Englishmen. I would willingly have given references, in addition, to that of Charles Blanc, as it is very clear and readable, and was charmingly illustrated by Flameng, but it seemed that a string of three references to every plate was likely to be confusing, especially as the names of the Frenchman and the German begin with the same letter.

II

The reputation of Rembrandt has undergone the most extreme vicissitudes. In his own life-time he rose from obscurity to a local and afterwards national celebrity, but sank down again, several years before his death, into the trying position of a neglected and unfashionable artist. "Often," says Vosmaer, "have I felt indignant at the small degree of enthusiasm manifested by his contemporaries." Vondel either really cared nothing for Rembrandt or affected complete indifference.

Another contemporary poet said that as Rembrandt found he could not equal Titian, Vandyke or Michael Angelo, he preferred to wander from the right path and become the first heretic in art rather than strengthen himself by following the most experienced. Houbraken speaks of the art of Rembrandt in the past tense, saying that it *had* (at one time) the success of novelty, it *was* a fashion, and artists had been obliged to imitate him in order to sell, even when their own manner of painting was far superior. Lairesse condemned Rembrandt and Lievens together, but, with a distant approach to generosity, went so far as to admit that Rembrandt's way of painting was "not absolutely bad." Some time after the artist's death came a reaction in his favour showing itself decidedly in the beginning of the eighteenth century by an extended appreciation in foreign countries. Still, throughout the eighteenth century, criticism was too subservient to classical authority to recognise Rembrandt with any complete cordiality, and if he was praised for some qualities he was condemned, with at least equal frankness, for the defects that accompanied them. Even so late in the century as the time of Barry, who began his Academy lectures in 1784, it was possible for him to speak of Rembrandt's "laborious, *ignorant* diligence," in rendering the "multiplied wrinkles and trifling peculiarities of the skin." He admitted the ability of Rembrandt in colouring and chiaroscuro but hated his most masterly style, condemning the "obtrusive, licentious, slovenly conduct of his pencil" as "not less disgusting than it is useless." Opie spoke of him as "foremost of those who in the opinion of some critics cut the knot instead of untying it, and burglariously entered the Temple of Fame by the window." Reynolds compared Poussin with Rembrandt as to their composition and management of light and shadow, adding that they "ran into contrary extremes and that it is difficult to determine which is the most reprehensible, both being equally distant from the demands of nature and the purposes of art." He admits that the pictures of Rembrandt may "not come amiss when mixed with the performances of artists of a more regular manner" Reynolds was just however (without being in the least enthusiastic) about both drawing and colour in *The Anatomical Lesson.* Fuseli appreciated Rembrandt better, classing him as a genius of the first rank "in whatever relates not to form." Again, Fuseli has an intelligent onslaught upon the topographic delineation of landscape and says that the landscape of Rembrandt "spurns all relation with this kind of map-work." He describes Rembrandt's figures as "uniform abstracts of lumpy or meagre deformity," but admits that, "form only excepted, he possessed every power that constitutes genius in art."

All these academical opinions, including the favourable one of Constable on Rembrandt's chiaroscuro picture of the Mill, refer to the master's work in painting, not to his etchings. One of the first English artists who took any special interest in the etchings was the elder Leslie, and he once wrote a short sentence of five lines about the services of photography in reproducing "these inestimable works." Mr. Ruskin once gave a foot-note, also of five lines, to Rembrandt's etchings, that appreciated the synthetic quality of the landscapes, and in the text of "Modern Painters," there are references to two plates, *The Presentation in the Temple* (B. 50. M. 243) and *The Shell* (B. 159. M. 290). I do not remember any other reference to the etchings in Mr. Ruskin's works except some depreciatory remarks upon their technique in a letter on the etchings of Mr. Ernest George.

In most of these instances of criticism, what strikes us is the remarkable coolness of the critics, their absence of anything approaching to enthusiasm. Those who appreciate in some degree the qualities of the master are not carried away by them, they have not the tone of critics speaking about an artist who has delighted them and whose defects they may be aware of but are willing to overlook ; they have the tone of men who, when they praise, do it from a wish to avoid injustice. Fuseli is hearty in praise and blame, Leslie and Constable praise heartily as far as they go, but are extremely laconical. The brevity of Mr. Ruskin is still more striking in a diffusely eloquent writer—six lines for the religious subjects, five for the landscapes, two for a study of still life !

The truth appears to be that the present splendour of Rembrandt's fame is more recent than we can easily realise. It has been due to several causes, distinct in themselves, but all operating together. The first is the complete extinction of classicism as an exclusive authority though it has happily survived, and with improved culture, as a taste. The second lies in the greater facilities for travelling which have enabled critics to see more of Rembrandt's whole performance and know him better, and the third is in the invention of certain processes of engraving in which photography does the drawing, though not the biting, and so far ensures a considerable degree of fidelity, as well as cheapness in the most recent reproductions. But these causes, potent as they are, would probably have had a less effect on Rembrandt's fame if they had not been accompanied, in all civilised countries, by a revival of the art of etching. The opinion amongst etchers which enthrones Rembrandt as the king of their craft is the most recent instance of perfect unanimity amongst people of all nationalities. As we all say that Phidias was the greatest sculptor, Homer the greatest epic poet, and Shakespeare the greatest dramatist, so are we all agreed upon the world-wide supremacy of Rembrandt. And the higher our appreciation of etching as essentially an artist's art the more exalted becomes the position of its greatest practitioner. I am told that, of late years, there has been some decline in the appreciation of etching. Perhaps it is no longer fashionable to pretend to be enchanted by its masterpieces, but these changes of surface-fashion have little to do with culture. The plain truth is that the etched work of Rembrandt is now intelligible to thousands, whereas in the beginning of the present century it was almost like an unknown tongue, or characters understood by few.

Another recent piece of good fortune for Rembrandt is that he has fallen into the hands of a competent biographer, Vosmaer, a writer entirely free from that credulity of mediocrity which makes it ever ready to accept the common calumnies against genius. The idlest and most ridiculous stories about Rembrandt had become traditional. Vosmaer showed that they had not, and that they could not have, any other foundation than the inventive spite of a great man's usual detractors. He showed us Rembrandt as he lived, a man of immense industry and the simplest tastes (with the one exception of a passion for works of art), a man whose force of character and courage in adversity immediately suggest to English readers the name of one great in another art who died like Rembrandt in harness and at Rembrandt's years, the artist who died at Abbotsford.

In his own lines of work there is no one in all history to be compared with Rembrandt; in artistic influence he has one equal, entirely unlike himself, and that is Raphael. It was not by accident that medallions of these two were put together on the cover of the *Portfolio*. They are the two most influential graphic artists of all time. Comte defined art as consisting in the three processes of observation, imitation, and idealisation. The three are common to both artists but in Rembrandt observation predominates, in Raphael idealisation. As for imitation they are alike in possessing the power of it and in using it more or less, but always subordinately to the artistic purpose. Raphael is called quite accurately in a certain sense, " the divine "; " the human " is an epithet that might, with equal justice, be applied to Rembrandt.

III

The date of the first etchings that have any date at all is the year 1628, when the artist was twenty-one years old. There are two signed etchings for that year. One of them, *An Old Woman's Head, full face, seen only to the Chin* (B. 352. M. 6.), is very simply etched, though drawn with easy skill, especially visible in the reserves of half-light in the shaded parts. It is already the work of an artist, but has no special distinction. The other little plate, *Bust of an Old Woman, lightly etched* (B. 354. M. 5), is much more than that; it is the work, already, of a great and most accomplished master. It was never afterwards surpassed, either in the penetrating observation of nature, or in delicate sufficiency of execution, by any subsequent work of Rembrandt himself, and it is almost impossible to believe that even so strong a natural genius as his could produce work of such rare excellence without years of previous practice, not only in drawing, but in actual work with the etching needle. He probably began to etch in his minority, making attempts that did not seem to him worth dating, then he did these things, and put not only his signature, but the year. However this may be, the fact is certain that at the age of twenty-one he had already mastered one of his several styles. I do not wish to exaggerate the matter, I do not believe that at twenty-one he could have got through such a task as the portrait of the Burgomaster Six, but he had already one of the strings to his bow.

At the date of these plates Rembrandt was living at his father's house in Leyden. He had been destined to a learned profession, but had not taken well to classical studies, and instead of proceeding with them had followed art in Van Swanenburch's studio for three years, which probably ended about 1620. After that he had been apprenticed to Pieter Lastman and stayed with him, according to Orlers, six months. It is believed that he returned to his father's house about 1623, and stayed there till 1630. At the date of the etchings that occupy us he had already painted a picture which is known and now at Stuttgart, and he had also taken his first pupil, Gerard Dow. Everything is rather early, rather precocious, with Rembrandt. He got up early in the morning of life, and set to work at a time when others are dreaming about what they intend to do. It has been assumed that the little etchings of 1628 were portraits of Rembrandt's mother, and they are so entered in Blanc's catalogue, but there is no evidence in favour of such an idea. According to Vosmaer the mother was about thirty-five years old at the date of Rembrandt's birth, consequently she would be about fifty-six when he came of age, but the old lady in the etching looks past seventy.[1]

There is just one etching for 1629, and that is an excellent proof of the tendency to vary his styles and make experiments, which was in Rembrandt's nature, and remained with him through life. The title of it in Mr. Middleton's catalogue is *Rembrandt, a Bust; supposed to be engraved on Pewter* (B. 336. M. 7.). It is a rough sketch in a bold and decided manner, without any attempt at delicacy of tone or even of line, but immense vivacity of handling, and the peculiarity of it is that some of the shading is done with a double point, as if two points had been tied together, which they probably were. Many etchers have tried that experiment for greater speed in shading, but it does not really advance matters very much, and Rembrandt never afterwards recurred to it.

The year 1630 is remarkable for a series of small plates, in which the artist amused himself in studying expression by assuming it in his own features. The practice may easily be represented as ridiculous, and has, no doubt, a ludicrous aspect, as it is difficult to think quite seriously of a grown man making faces, as children do, before a glass. It has been

---

[1] Many women after seventy are better preserved than Rembrandt's old lady; Queen Victoria is an instance, and in quiet middle-class life good preservation is by no means rare. This Dutchwoman, tranquil and fairly well off, might very well be eighty. I have known a younger-looking lady at ninety-three.

done occasionally by modern actors for instantaneous photography, and
with this result, that when the costume is changed at the same time as
the expression the original human being becomes unrecognisable. Rembrandt himself is not always immediately recognised in these etchings,
but we get accustomed to the changes in his physiognomy, in his head-
gear, and in the length of his hair. We have him "with an open
mouth" (B. 13. M. 22.); "with an air of grimace" (B. 10. M. 23.);
"with haggard eyes" (B. 320. M. 24.); and "laughing" (B. 316.
M. 25.). These little plates, and others, probably of the same date, or
very near it, are executed with a fine point, and are distinguished by an
extreme manual facility. The evident speed of their execution does not,
however, prevent the artist from noticing the most minute truths of form
and of light and shade, as, for example, in the learnedly reserved reflec-

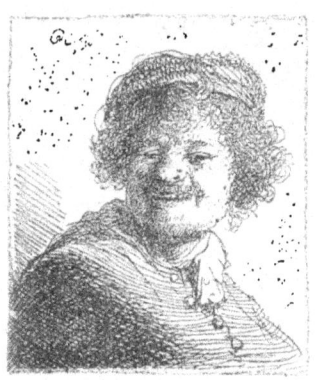

Rembrandt, Full Face, Laughing.
B. 316. M. 25.

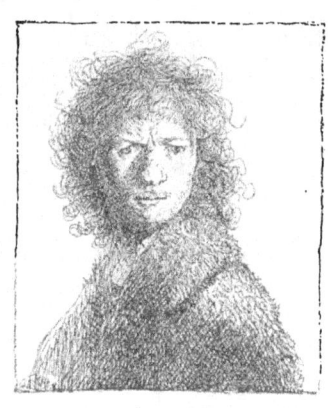

Rembrandt with an Air of Grimace.
B. 10. M. 23.

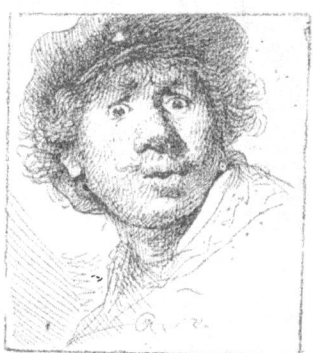

Rembrandt with Haggard Eyes.
B. 320. M. 24.

tions in the shading of *Rembrandt with an open Mouth* (B. 13. M. 22.).
There may be haste in such work as this, but there is no carelessness, and
as for vitality it is superabundant, both in the subjects and the execution.

In the same year, 1630, Rembrandt made two serious etchings of
himself, one "with curly hair rising into a tuft over the right eye"
(B. 27. M. 26.) the other "with fur cap and light dress" (B. 24. M. 27.).
Both these plates are very lightly sketched in the manner that the French
call "croquis." The one with the fur cap is a pleasant and probably
very truthful likeness of the artist at the age of twenty-three, without

any flattery as to form, but having the air of a young man at the same time very intelligent and perfectly satisfied with himself. The other gives a fine idea of Rembrandt's abundant head of hair which resembles as to quantity the wigs of the eighteenth century. It may be that he sometimes added in his paintings and etchings to the liberal gifts of nature, as in portraits of the same year the hair is at one time prodigious and at another ordinary. For example, in *Rembrandt with Haggard Eyes*, there is not enough of it to attract attention.

Rembrandt now began his long series of etchings of scriptural subjects. One, dated 1630, is a *Jesus Disputing with the Doctors* (B. 66. M. 177.), a small plate, delicately etched, but very grandly conceived, and another of the same year is *The Presentation with the Angel* (B. 51. M. 178.), called so because an angel with wings appears over the left shoulder of Anna the prophetess. Like the *Jesus Disputing*, this plate is of small dimen-sions and slight rather than powerful execution.

It seems highly probable that Rembrandt began to etch beggars very early in life, as the style that he adopted for that class of subject was quite fully developed in 1630, and there are several etchings of that year, dated, which are not inferior in execution to the numerous beggar subjects of later years. There are also some good portrait studies, for example, *An Old Man with a Large Beard, the Shoulders lower than the Ears* (B. 309, M. 31), which is one of Rembrandt's finest studies of old age.

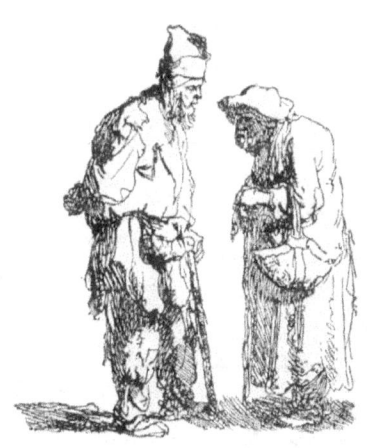

Two Beggars, a Man and a Woman Conversing. B. 164. M. 37.

There is the *Profile of a Bald Man* (B. 292. M. 39.) and the *Portrait of a Man with a broad-brimmed Hat and a Ruff* which is unquestionably one of the most entirely satisfactory of Rembrandt's simpler little plates (B. 311. M. 28.).

I have dwelt in some detail on these plates because they have a special interest as showing what a good start Rembrandt made in etching, and how early in life. We have now to remember that at the age of twenty-one he executed the little plate of the old lady, which has never been surpassed in its own way, and that at twenty-three he had tried his hand, with rare success, on a variety of subjects and in three or four different styles. He was already in the peculiar situation of an artist who has left himself no room for improvement except in attempting art of another kind, and in overcoming new, though possibly not greater difficulties.

With the exception of the six months spent in the studio of Pieter Lastman, Rembrandt had hitherto remained entirely with his parents at Leyden, as his three years' pupilage with Swanenburch, then a Leyden artist, does not imply any change of residence. Rembrandt's youth had been free from every care but that of his own progress in art. His parents were in easy circumstances in the burgher class

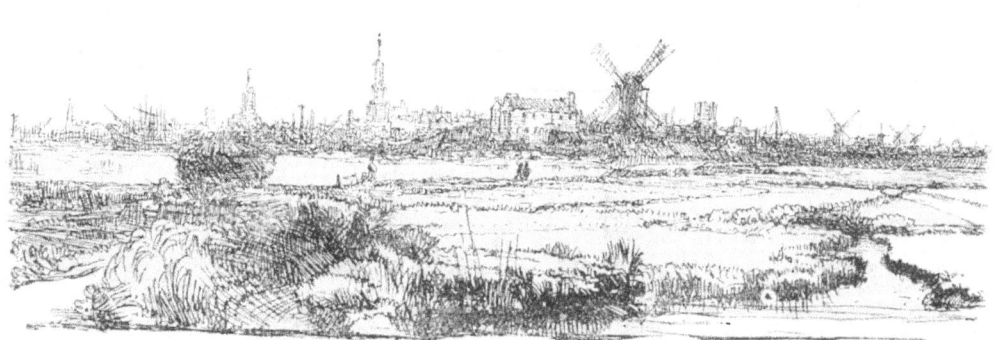

View of Amsterdam. B. 210. M. 304.

and if he had not received a full classical education it was only because he had not taken to it. Born for the graphic arts, he had taken to painting and etching with the utmost interest and immediate success. This justified him in establishing himself as an artist with a house and studio of his own, and he selected Amsterdam rather than Leyden as a place of residence, though the choice involved a separation from

his father, who died about two years later, from his mother, who
lived on for ten years, and from his four brothers and two sisters
who were all living at that time. Settled in Amsterdam in 1630,
Rembrandt resumed his etching. The plates dated 1631 include
twenty-seven portraits and studies, one "fancy composition," if a
single figure deserves the title, but no religious subject. This year
the portraits include five of himself, of which the most perfect,
technically, is *Rembrandt with Round Fur Cap, full face* (B. 16.
M. 45.) but that is in the earlier style. The desire for new con-
quests is shown in the larger *Rembrandt with Broad Hat and
Embroidered Mantle* (B. 7. M. 52.) in which the etcher has laboriously
aimed at high finish and rich textures without, however, abandoning
his former delicate treatment of light passages as in the collar and
the lighted side of the face and hair. It may be noted as a sign of
increasing prosperity and self-respect that the young painter, instead
of pulling faces in the glass, now poses before it with the air and
costume of a well-bred gentleman. Another very fine portrait of this
time is that of the *Man with a Short Beard and Embroidered Cloak*
(B. 263. M. 77.), full of clear and decided drawing without any over-
finish. The student may observe how completely explanatory, with few
lines, is the treatment of the costume. Rembrandt still retains his
former interest in old age and proves it by a wonderfully beautiful
Bust of an Old Man with a Long Beard (B. 260. M. 62.). The
wrinkled forehead would no doubt have been accepted by Barry as a
proof of Rembrandt's "ignorant diligence" in copying "the multiplied
wrinkles and trifling peculiarities of the skin." This is one of the most
perfect of Rembrandt's lighter and more delicate etchings, and there is
another charming little sketch plate of an old bearded man with the
date of 1631 (B. 315. M. 63.). In this year Rembrandt went on with
his series of beggars, but without any change of style, and etched in the
same light manner a clever plate of very small dimensions known as
The Little Polander (B. 142. M. 79.). One of the most important
works of the year was the portrait of *Rembrandt's Mother, her Hand
resting upon her Breast* (B. 348. M. 55.). This etching belongs to
the same class of serious, highly finished, and dignified works as the
portrait of the artist himself with the *Broad Hat and Embroidered*

Mantle. It was a new style with Rembrandt then and these works have an air which implies that he took a certain pride in it. Certainly this portrait of his mother is one of the most beautiful etchings he ever produced. The contrasts of delicacy and strength of line in flesh and costume are extreme but never offensive. They occur always in the right place and however easy the workmanship there is no carelessness.

For the year 1632 there is nothing dated, in the way of studies and portraits, except a vastly broad figure of a Persian " swell " (there is no other word for him) who goes swaggering along with cloak, and fringes, and medal, and cane, and plume! It is a charming example of the serio-comical, admirably etched in a light incisive way (B. 152. M. 91.). The same year is marked by a return to religious subjects in a St. Jerome, praying passionately, *St. Jerome Kneeling, an Arched Print* (B. 101. M. 183.). Notwithstanding the difference of subject, St. Jerome is etched in the same light and clever manner as the distinguished Persian. This, too, is the year of *The Rat Killer* (B. 121. M. 261.), one of Rembrandt's characteristic plates of popular subjects reminding us in that respect of Ostade, and also in the complete absence of local colour. The execution is like that of some of the beggar series but not so lively as the best of them. It is a complete Dutch picture as to composition, though the light-and-shade is little more than indicated.

I have never admired the portrait of 1633, *Rembrandt with a Scarf round his Neck* (B. 17, M. 99). The face is almost entirely in shade, except a little sunshine on the left cheek, and as the shading is heavy, coarse, and over-bitten, it looks as if the original had had his face blackened.

It is most difficult to give a satisfactory account of Rembrandt's etched work for the year 1633, as it so happens that some of the most important parts of what is attributed to him for that year are subjects of doubt and discussion, and must therefore be reserved for later consideration. There is no evidence that Rembrandt made any progress as an etcher in that year. What was intended to be a very important plate, a great *Descent from the Cross*, was entirely ruined in the biting, ruined past redemption, so that after two or three trial proofs the plate was abandoned. A second plate of the same composition appears to have been

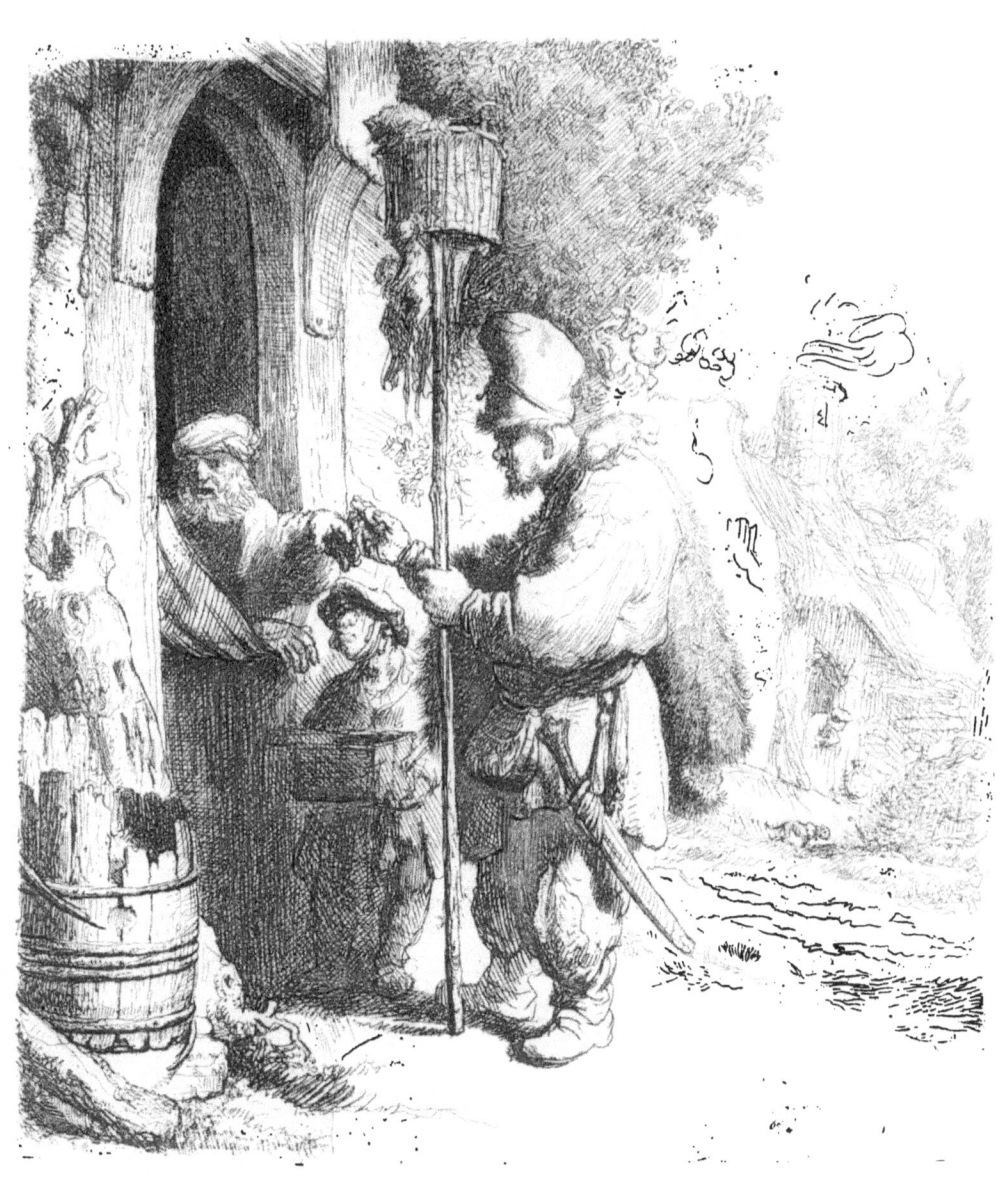

etched by another hand. We know from the number of pictures signed by Rembrandt at this time or soon after that he was most industriously occupied with painting, and he now began, probably for commercial reasons, to make compositions for large plates full of tiresome work and for which he would naturally be tempted to employ assistants. The experience of all etchers has shown that the big commercial plate is an artistic error, whatever may be its immediate pecuniary advantages. There is, however, a very little plate, *An Old Woman etched no lower than the Chin* (B. 351, M. 101), which is a return, without any visible improvement, to the artist's simplest and most elementary style of five years before.

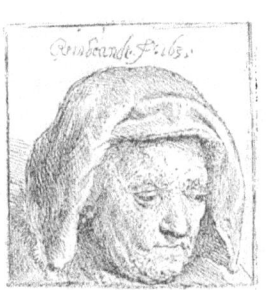

*An Old Woman etched no lower than the Chin.
B. 351. M. 101.*

The production of large commercial plates, as well as the painting of many pictures about this time, may have been connected with ideas of marriage in obedience to the Shakespearian rule, " Put money in thy purse." In June 1634 Rembrandt married Saskia van Ulenburgh at Bilt in Friesland. She was a young lady of good family, and although Rembrandt was not in the least worldly or what is called a " society man," still, as his marriage improved his social position, he may have been tempted to some display about this time. It was a very brilliant marriage for a young artist. Vosmaer tells us that Saskia gave Rembrandt admission " into a distinguished family, whose members illustrated the magistrature, science, literature, and the arts." She also brought Rembrandt a good fortune, and there is evidence that the marriage was a happy one.

There are uncertainties and disappointments in etching even for the most experienced masters, and one of the worst plates that Rembrandt ever made, if, indeed, he did entirely execute it with his own hand, is the portrait of *Jan Sylvius* (B. 266. M. 110.), that of 1634, which is not to be confounded with the fine later portrait of Sylvius preaching, executed four years later. The first Sylvius does not show Rembrandt's usual skill in drawing (look at the right nostril and the wooden hands) whilst the shading is heavy and of poor quality, being without any effectual varieties of tone, texture, and handling. Admiration of bad work like this, whether sincere or feigned, only diminishes the value of that which is rightly given to good examples of the art. It is interesting to observe that in the same year (1634) Rembrandt recurred to the very simplest and most elementary (but often most satisfactory) kind of etching, clear line and plain shading, in some studies of beggars which are admirable examples of such work, to be recommended to the attention of all practical beginners.

The year 1634 is that of the very celebrated etching called *The Great Jewish Bride* (B. 340. M. 108.). This title has nothing to do with the bigness of the bride herself; it is merely used to distinguish the plate from a smaller one of another person. M. Charles Blanc made it out to his own satisfaction that this is really a portrait of Saskia, Rembrandt's wife, his strongest argument being that the plate was executed in the year of his marriage. The other argument, based on likeness to known portraits of Saskia, is untenable. The two women are not of the same feminine type. The Saskia who is in the plate called *Rembrandt and his Wife* (B. 19. M. 128.) is a bright-looking, intelligent woman, and so is the lady, evidently the same person, in *Rembrandt's Wife and Five other Heads* (B. 365. M. 129.). The Jewish Bride, on the other hand, has certainly less than the usual intelligence of her race. She is a fine woman, physically, and she has magnificent hair, but she is only a fine woman and Saskia is much more. Besides, the Jewish lady looks as if she could be bad-tempered, which Saskia does not. The Jewess has a low forehead, a large ugly mouth with protruding lower lip, and a very dark complexion; Saskia's forehead is high, her mouth small and pretty, and her complexion fair. M. Charles Blanc believed that the uppermost of the *Three Heads of Women* (B. 367. M. 115.) had at least been suggested by Saskia. This seems very probable, the face is pleasant and intelligent.

The Great Jewish Bride, in its finished state, is an attempt at complete tonality. It is more successful in that respect than the first portrait of Sylvius, but I may be excused for preferring the costume portrait which Mr. Middleton calls *Portrait, Unknown, of a Man with a Sabre* (B. 23. M. 111.), but which Mr. Haden and others have believed to be Rembrandt himself. M. Charles Blanc was disposed to abandon this idea, as there is not much likeness to other self-portraits of the master and there is a wart on this face that does not occur in the others. Blanc saw a likeness to the Duke of Gueldres, but the search of an original is unnecessary, as the etching is most probably a fancy piece, only bearing some resemblance to Rembrandt himself, without pretending to be a likeness. It is very cleverly executed. The shade on the face is too black, which may probably be accounted for by the original intention

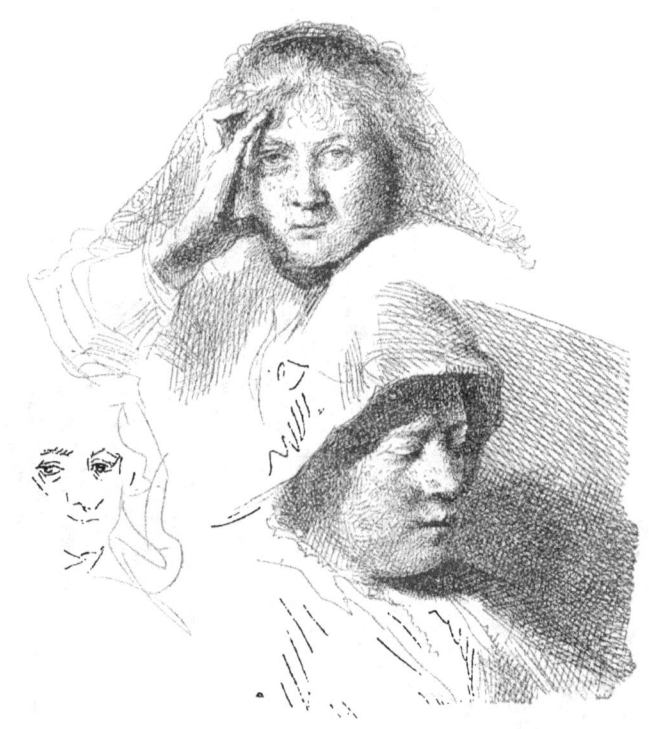

Three Heads of Women. B. 367. M. 115.

to use the copper as an ornamental plate on a box rather than for printing. There was, however, in Rembrandt's work at this time a decided tendency to over-shading, the consequence of those experiments in full tonality which all etchers seem to be, at one time in their lives, tempted to make. A charming plate of this year, *A Young Woman reading* (B. 345, M. 109.), is injured by too great darkness and heaviness in the shading of the face. In the same year, 1634, we find two small plates of religious subjects, *The Samaritan Woman—at the Ruins* (B. 71.

M. 195.) and *Jesus and the Disciples at Emmaus* (B. 88. M. 194.) in which full tonality is not attempted.   There are, however, some reasons for believing that Rembrandt borrowed the conception of these works from other artists.   Mr. Haden suggests Dow for the *Samaritan Woman. The Martyrdom of St. Stephen* (B. 97. M. 197) is a work of the same class, well composed, brilliant and effective, but far from being one of the

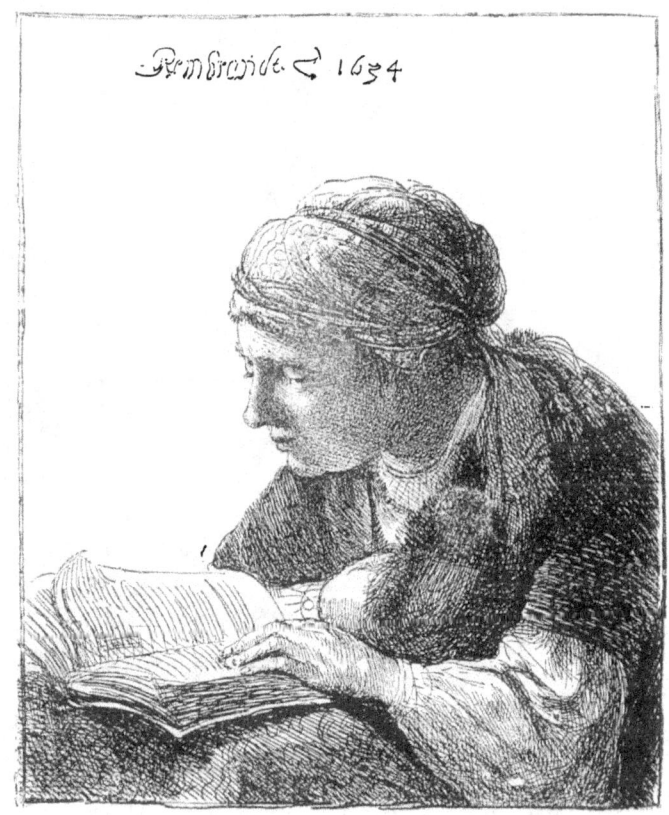

A Young Woman reading.   B. 345. *M.* 109.

best drawn amongst Rembrandt's etchings ; the lower part of St. Stephen's body is very difficult to defend or account for satisfactorily.   There is bad drawing, too, in the poor plate of *Jesus Christ Driving out the Money Changers* (B. 69. M. 198.), of which the principal figure is borrowed from Albert Dürer, whilst the miserable cow, besides being much too small, is hardly better as a study of animal life than the scared cattle in the large plate of *The Angel appearing to the Shepherds* (B. 44. M. 191.).   The

truth is that Rembrandt was a most unequal artist and that there is no
regularity in his onward course. He was always ready to etch with a
new aim and adopt some style in which he had not much previous experience, the attempt being sometimes successful and sometimes partially
or completely a failure. We have seen how he attempted complete
tonality in *The Great Jewish Bride* and woodcut effects in three of the
smaller religious compositions. It is strange that the author of these
plates could and did, nearly at the same date, etch such a marvellously
perfect little masterpiece as *The Mountebank* (B. 129.
M. 117.). The execution is most intelligent, not
a line too many nor a shade too dark, and no one
doubts that it is by the hand of Rembrandt,
though the original idea of the subject has been
attributed to Jan Van de Velde. The well-
known portrait of *Johannes Uijtenbogaerd* (B. 279.
M. 114.) is a realisation of that complete scale
of lights and darks which Rembrandt had for
some time, in an intermittent way, been aiming
at. It is very fortunate that the desire for depth
and richness did not lead, in this instance, to any
overshading of the face which is delicately and
most observantly drawn. There is an early state
of the plate before the darkening of the background. As in the *Uijtenbogaerd* the scheme of

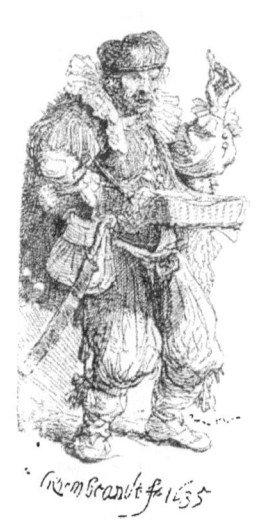

The Mountebank.
B. 129. *M.* 117.

light and dark is a bright centre surrounded by dark shades, so in
The Pancake Woman (B. 124. M. 264.) the scheme is a dark figure
surrounded by lighter ones and by a light background. The style is
as different as possible from that of the other plates of the year 1635.
The idea and composition are hardly like Rembrandt and have been
credited to the original author of *The Mountebank*.

Rembrandt continued the practice of his lighter style in 1636. For
example, the portrait of *Menasseh Ben Israel* (B. 269. M. 127.) is an excellent example of plain straightforward etching in clearly bitten black line.
I take the liberty of recommending it as a good model for amateurs;
if they think such etching does not look delicate enough they can work
over it, sparingly and judiciously, in dry point. Mr. Middleton says

that Menasseh Ben Israel " was one of Rembrandt's most intimate friends, living near him in the Breedstraat. He early established his reputation as an author: and it shows the high estimation in which he was held

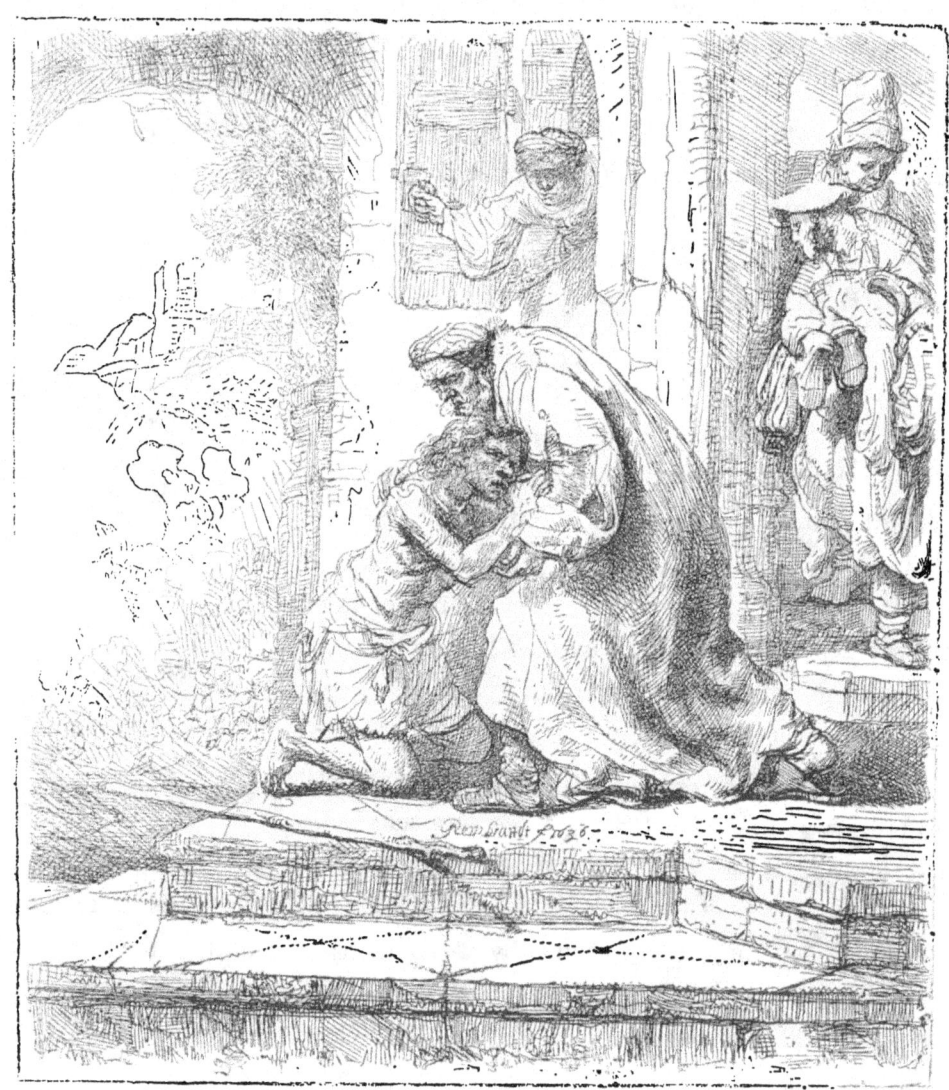

THE PRODIGAL SON. B. 91. M. 201.

by his co-religionists that he was deputed by them to undertake a mission to the Protector Cromwell to obtain from him the recall of the Jews to England."

A very important little work from the biographical point of view is the etching of *Rembrandt and his Wife* (B. 19. M. 128.). By an effect of what is called " exaggerated perspective," [1] Rembrandt's face appears enormous in comparison with that of Saskia. It is pleasant to know that she was a good wife to him, and that their short married life was a happy one. She appears again in the plate of sketches called *Rembrandt's Wife and Five other Heads* (B. 365. M. 129.). They are all masterly sketches without more than a clear suggestion of light and shade. The year 1636 is also the date of *The Prodigal Son* (B. 91. M. 201.), an etching in Rembrandt's simplest manner, not agreeable at first sight, as there is little charm of execution and the personages, especially the wretched youth himself, are ill-favoured, but the subject has never been treated with deeper imaginative sympathy. The repentant humility of the son and the affectionate forgiving tenderness of the father are enough to disarm criticism.

IV

The years through which we are now passing were the happiest of Rembrandt's life. The great fertility of his mind and hand and a habit of regarding an " old master " as a very experienced man may easily make us forget that in 1637 Rembrandt was only thirty years old and his beloved Saskia only twenty-five. Yet if Rembrandt had died at that time his name would still have survived as that of a great master. He had already done some of his very best work both in painting and etching. He had painted *The Anatomical Lesson* five years before and, before that or after, many a picture now in the most famous collections of the world. As for what he had done in etching, I need only say that the plates I have mentioned give an inadequate idea as I have restricted myself, hitherto, to those which bear a date. Rembrandt was a man of great courage, great fortitude, so that he bore

---

[1] The expression is not accurate but we know what is meant by it. When the draughtsman is too near to the nearest objects which he represents, he may draw them quite truthfully and accurately and yet make them look too big relatively to what is behind them. This is a very common fault even in the present day and in the works of the most distinguished draughtsmen, who do not seem to perceive how objectionable it is.

well in later life the stress and strain of sorrow, solitude, and adversity, but it is pleasant to think that he lived the golden days of his life's summer at Amsterdam with Saskia, a summer of fame and love, of pecuniary ease and peace, surrounded by works of art, and in a large richly furnished mansion which we may be sure that Saskia, as a Dutch lady of good family, would keep for him in the most exquisite cleanliness and order. It is true that there had been changes in the old paternal home at Leyden. Rembrandt's father, Harmen, had died about 1632, his mother lost three of her children before 1640 and lived with her youngest daughter Lijsbeth. The eldest son Adriaen, who was seventeen years older than Rembrandt, kept on the paternal mill. Such was the situation of Rembrandt and his family when he was thirty years old. He was already a father, his son Rumbartus having been born in December 1635.

Three of the most perfect of Rembrandt's smaller plates belong to the year 1637. We have *Abraham sending away Hagar and Ishmael* (B. 30. M. 204.), an exquisite work by no means overcharged with labour, and not pretending to be in full tone, yet extremely rich in materials and in the abundant but not obtrusive indication of details. The dramatic action of the figures is very finely conceived, especially that of the majestic, unpitying patriarch. In the same year we find a portrait, also of the patriarchal type, *An Old Man wearing a rich Velvet Cap* (B. 313. M. 131.) highly finished, but not over-shaded and well preserving the different qualities of flesh, and hair, and dress in which it is much superior, for example, to the *Young Woman reading* (B. 345. M. 109.) though that is also, in other ways, an excellent etching. A very admirable portrait of 1637 is *A Young Man seated, turned to the Left* (B. 268. M. 132.). This is called in the French catalogues "Jeune homme assis et réfléchissant" because he has a serious expression of thoughtful meditation. Without being so highly finished as the portrait just described it is equally sound in workmanship and unquestionably one of the most faultless pieces in the whole collection. It always strongly reminds me of Francia's absorbing and entrancing picture of the melancholy young man in the Louvre. The reader will remember that in 1636 Rembrandt made several sketches of heads on the same copper, including a pretty portrait of Saskia. He repeated the experiment in

1637 with one head as a study of sleep. The etching is entered in Mr. Middleton's catalogue as *Three Heads of Women, One asleep* (B. 368. M. 130.). The plate is not quite so light and elegant in touch and treatment as that of the preceding year, nor are the models so agreeable, but the sleeping woman is most closely observed.

I hope the reader will not take it as evidence of disrespect towards our first parents if I say that it is impossible to look at Rembrandt's etching of *Adam and Eve* (B. 38. M. 206.) without a lively sense of the ludicrous. Rembrandt did not flatter our vanity by telling us that we had such ancestors as these. So remote are they from all our notions of what is comely in the human form, that one regrets the impossibility (whilst remaining faithful to the text) of providing them with decent habiliments. Even M. Dutuit, with all his admiration for Rembrandt, admits that " Adam et Ève ont réellement une figure repoussante." So, indeed, they have, and yet, in spite of their ugliness, the etching as a whole is far from being destitute of artistic beauty. It is finely composed and well lighted. The dragon that represents the serpent is grandly conceived, and the attitudes of Adam and Eve would have been appreciated in handsomer bodies. The manual execution of the simple linear work all about the tree and dragon is strong and masterly, bearing some resemblance to the pen-drawing of Titian.

A less questionable scriptural subject of this year is *Joseph telling his Dreams* (B 37. M. 205.), a rich little composition, as the subject was a good pretext for crowding many figures into a small space. This etching is closely related in style to such plates as the little one of *The Disciples at Emmaus* and *The Stoning of St. Stephen*. The portraits of the year include *Rembrandt in Mezetin Cap and Feather* (B. 20. M. 134.), a plate which looks less effective than many others because there are no intense blacks, and because it is almost uniformly etched with a fine point throughout, but there is much beautiful drawing in it, and much character, and Mr. Middleton observes that, " when rich in tone and exquisitely clear, as in the superb impression at Amsterdam, it is a work of singular beauty."

There is a well-known little etching of 1638, which has been called by two different names, *Saint Catherine*, and also *The Little Jewish Bride* (B. 342. M. 135.). It is pretty, both from the pleasing character of the model and the absence of all pretension in her pose. The execution is equally unpretending, the very simplicity of treatment and biting having led to a certain wiriness in the hair. Some believe that this is a study of Saskia, but this girlish face is not like that of the clever-looking young woman in the plate of sketches (B. 365. M. 129.), and, for my part, I remain incredulous. The title *Saint Catherine* was suggested by the wheel in the corner.

V.

Rembrandt's family increased in the year 1638, when Saskia had a little girl whom they called Cornelya, but she lived only from the twenty-second of July to the sixteenth of August.

Two changes of residence may also be noted, but for these we have not precise dates. In February 1636 he had quitted the Breedstraat, and was living in the Niewe Doelstraat. In January 1639 he lived on the interior quay of the Amstel in a house called the Suijkerbackerij We do not exactly know at what date he left this residence for his fine mansion in the Jodenbreedstraat.

The year 1639 is of great importance in the history of Rembrandt's career as an etcher. He had already done such excellent work that it seems as if improvement must have been impossible, but his experiments in various directions appear to have left a temporary conviction in his mind that etchings loaded with heavy work, like *The Great Jewish Bride*, were not the best adapted to expression in this art, and that a lighter style was preferable. Nevertheless, his experience in various styles, even in the heaviest (as in the background and lower part of Johannes Uijtenbogaerd) had increased his power of execution. The portrait of himself, *Rembrandt Leaning on a Stone Sill* (B. 21. M. 137.), is a splendid example of high culture in the art of etching, going far enough in the darks for the expression of power but completely, even in the darkest parts, avoiding the mere thickness and density of printing ink, whilst the treble notes of this linear music are light and clear and faithfully true in tone. Observe how greatly superior is the shading on this face to that of *Rembrandt with a Scarf round his Neck* (B. 17. M. 99.) or to the face-blackening of *Rembrandt with Bushy Hair and*

Small White Collar (B. 1. M. 51.) or to that of *Rembrandt in a Fur Cap and Dark Dress* (B. 6. M. 17.). The hair, too, is treated with great skill, and in such a manner as to convey at the same time the sense of mass and a certain vigour of individual growth in the hairs themselves. It is far better, for example, than the coarse hair of *The Great Jewish Bride*, and, in itself, a sufficient answer to Mr. Ruskin's statement that nobody had ever etched hair. It would be interesting to see an attempt to copy it with a burin. The technical excellence of this plate is accompanied by a most animated expression of countenance; not histrionic, as in the studies of assumed expressions, but that of a keen intelligence in its ordinary condition of observant wakefulness.

Another great masterpiece, small and slight as it may look, is *Youth Surprised by Death* (B. 109. M. 265.), a plate very lightly sketched but with a rare degree of delicacy and elegance both in the execution and in the conception of the subject. No one able to feel the charm of first-rate sketching would wish to see a line added to such a performance as this, or a shade of it darkened.

And lastly, this year 1639 brings us to the magnificent *Death of the Virgin* (B. 99. M. 207.), which if the dimensions of the copper, the nobility and grandeur of the conception, and beauty of style in execution are all to be taken into account, is certainly the greatest of all Rembrandt's works. It is not so popular as *Jesus Christ healing the Sick* (the Hundred Guilder Print) for which one reason may be that it has not so striking an effect of chiaroscuro, but it is equal to it both in human sympathy and in picturesque treatment, and superior in the superb energy of its most masterly style. I am well aware that such a display of manual power, of executive *bravura*, is incompatible with the perfection of form, and I know that the shapes of the angels will not bear scrutiny, still there is much wonderful drawing in the Virgin herself, and in the people round the death-bed.

VI

The year 1640 is marked in the biography of Rembrandt by his mother's death, which took place in the month of September, at Leyden He had a second daughter this year, who was baptized in July, and received the name of the first, Cornelya.   There is no dated etching of 1640 worth special mention except the *Portrait, Unknown, of an Old Man with a Divided Fur Cap* (B. 265. M. 145.), a work of great dignity and beauty, but not likely to be popular from the absence of vigorous blacks.   It is, however, admirably drawn, and though the distinctions of tone and local colour are slight this etching is one of the most faultless that Rembrandt ever executed, and perfectly harmonious in its own key.

This brings us to the year 1641 when, in all probability, Rembrandt removed to his fine house in the Jodenbreedstraat.   My limits are too restricted for more than an occasional glance at the artist's private life. With the help of the inventory of Rembrandt's effects, Vosmaer made a most interesting description of the interior of the house with its well-furnished entrance hall where there were six Spanish chairs and twenty-four pictures, then the antechamber full of pictures including a Palma Vecchio, a Bassano, and a Raphael; there were also a mirror in an ebony frame, a big walnut table with a Tournay table-cover, and Spanish chairs with cushions in green velvet.   Beyond this room again was another room that interests us particularly, for here was Rembrandt's private press.   However, it was not a bare and simple printing room, but rather a picture gallery, including, as in Turner's gallery two hundred years later, only too many of the prolific artist's unsold works, now of inestimable value, but along with these many pictures by other masters. Here he had his etching-table with the usual shade to temper the light, and his oaken printing press, which was, I fear, but a clumsy piece of mechanism in comparison with the iron machines that our scientific makers construct for us to-day.   Then there was a general sitting-room, also full of pictures, by Rembrandt himself and others, including a Raphael and large Giorgione.

So much for the ground floor.   Above it were a suite of rooms more like a museum than apartments in a private mansion.   There was a rich

collection of paintings, sculpture, casts, porcelain, and armour, besides
many natural objects that had a picturesque interest for the master, such
as plants, shells, and stuffed birds, in a word everything that could charm
or amuse the most cultivated visual sense. There was a smaller room
near to this, also a museum, and then came the studio adorned with
a quantity of arms and costumes, a vestibule with lions' skins, and a small
study rich in pictures. The collection of books consisted chiefly of
volumes of drawings and engravings, abundant enough to prove the keen
interest that Rembrandt took in the works of others.

The reader may imagine him living in this palace of art with his dear
Saskia, the steps of Death, however rapidly advancing, as yet inaudible in
the distance.

The etchings of 1641 are remarkable for an extreme diversity of
manner and also, with one notable exception, for a general appearance of
haste as if their author had been too much occupied with his painting to
bestow much time upon his secondary art. The exception to this rule is
the highly finished portrait of *Cornelis Anslo* (B. 271. M. 146.) which
may have been taken as a model by our modern etchers from pictures.
It was, in fact, executed deliberately from a drawing. Another attempt
at full tone, but much coarser in execution, is a black little plate of this
year entitled *The Schoolmaster* (B. 128. M. 271.). It is a night effect—
a schoolmaster with several children arriving at the door of a house and a
woman is speaking to him from the inside. What light there is comes
from the interior.

Amongst the etchings of 1641 is a curiously mediæval-looking
Portrait of a Man with a Crucifix and Chain (B. 261. M. 147.). It is not
merely that the costume is of a time anterior to that of Rembrandt, but
he has adopted an archaic interpretation of life. In works really his own
there is always expression of some kind, but here the face is as void of
mind as it is of beauty. The same model, in the same costume, but less
elaborated, reappears in *A Man Playing Cards* (B. 136. M. 269.), a rapid
sketch on copper. Another sketch is that of *The Virgin and Child in the
Clouds* (B. 61. M. 211.), which only proves how little the genius of
Rembrandt was fitted to rise above the earth and its familiar realities, and
the same may be said of *The Angel ascending from Tobit and his Family*
(B. 43. M. 213.), where the substantial legs and feet of the angel in the

air (all that is seen of him) inevitably suggest those of Harlequin leaping through the window.

The Baptism of the Eunuch (B. 98. M. 210.) is a sketch principally *au trait*, and *The Large Lion Hunt* (B. 114. M. 272.) is a far swifter sketch of a most spirited composition, in the execution of which the

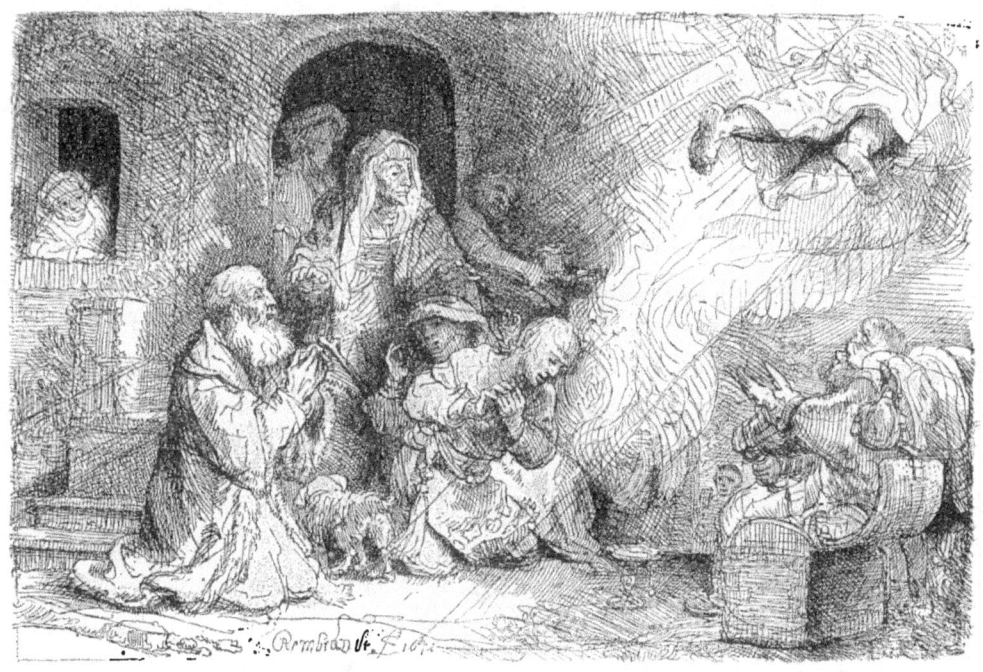

The Angel ascending from Tobit and his Family. B. 43. M. 213.

artist has not given himself time enough for any accuracy in form. *Three Oriental Figures* (B. 118. M. 212.[1]) may be taken as an example

---

[1] In Mr. Middleton's catalogue this plate is entered as *Jacob and Laban*, a title given to it by M. Charles Blanc. It has, however, been cogently pointed out by M. Dutuit that the incident which Blanc supposed to have been illustrated by this etching occurred in camp life. Laban had followed Jacob, who had pitched his tent in the mount of Gilead ; Laban stopped and encamped near him, and then went to Jacob's tent to remonstrate with him for having stolen his goods. In the etching we see nothing of the picturesque of camp life, which Rembrandt, who was a close reader of the Bible, and a great lover of the picturesque, would have been sure to seize upon. Instead of that, we have a house without even any signs of travelling, only three people in Eastern costume who have come to speak to the occupant. I called the plate " Jacob and Laban " in *Etching and Etchers*, merely from deference to Charles Blanc. However, I

of simple linear work, with a suggestion of shade, the whole without any attempt at delicacy in biting, so that the plate remained in a good condition for printing even to our own time, and I had an edition taken from it in the year 1868.

The activity of Rembrandt's observant mind was always likely to lead him in new directions, and it is not surprising to find him, in 1641, turning his attention to landscape, for which he had a strong natural sentiment. Two plates of this year, *A Large Landscape with a Dutch Hay Barn* (B. 225. M. 306.) and *A Large Landscape with a Mill-sail* (B. 226. M. 307.) are of more importance, perhaps, as examples of Rembrandt's skill in the treatment of picturesque rustic buildings than as interpretations of pure nature, but although the buildings predominate the foregrounds are treated with a lively sense of beauty in vegetation and the distances are delightful. Rembrandt had already fixed, in its essentials, his method of interpretation in landscape. Another plate of 1641, *The Mill, often called Rembrandt's Mill*[1] (B. 233. M. 305.), is a proof of his interest in picturesque buildings with a distance of very slight importance, though not without its own decided character.

VII

In the year 1641 Rembrandt had a son, Titus, baptized in the December[2] of that year.

In the month of June, 1642, he lost his beloved Saskia, who died at the early age of twenty-nine years and eleven months, her husband being then within a few weeks of thirty-five. So the fine house, with all its treasures, was made desolate, and the still young widower was left with his little child Titus.[3] Courage and strength of will remained to him, but the perfection of his happiness was gone for ever.

mentioned the other title also. The plain truth is that nobody knows what Rembrandt intended to illustrate in this plate, or whether he had any intention at all, beyond the mere grouping of some picturesque personages.

[1] M. Dutuit says, "This mill is not that where Rembrandt is said to have been born. We know positively that he was not born in a building of this kind. It is thought that this mill was situated at Carwijk, on the Rhine."

[2] Vosmaer says December in his text and September in the pedigree.

[3] Vosmaer does not give the dates of death for the first boy Rumbartus, and the

The dated etchings for this sad year are neither numerous nor important. There is a *St. Jerome: in Rembrandt's dark Manner* (B. 105.

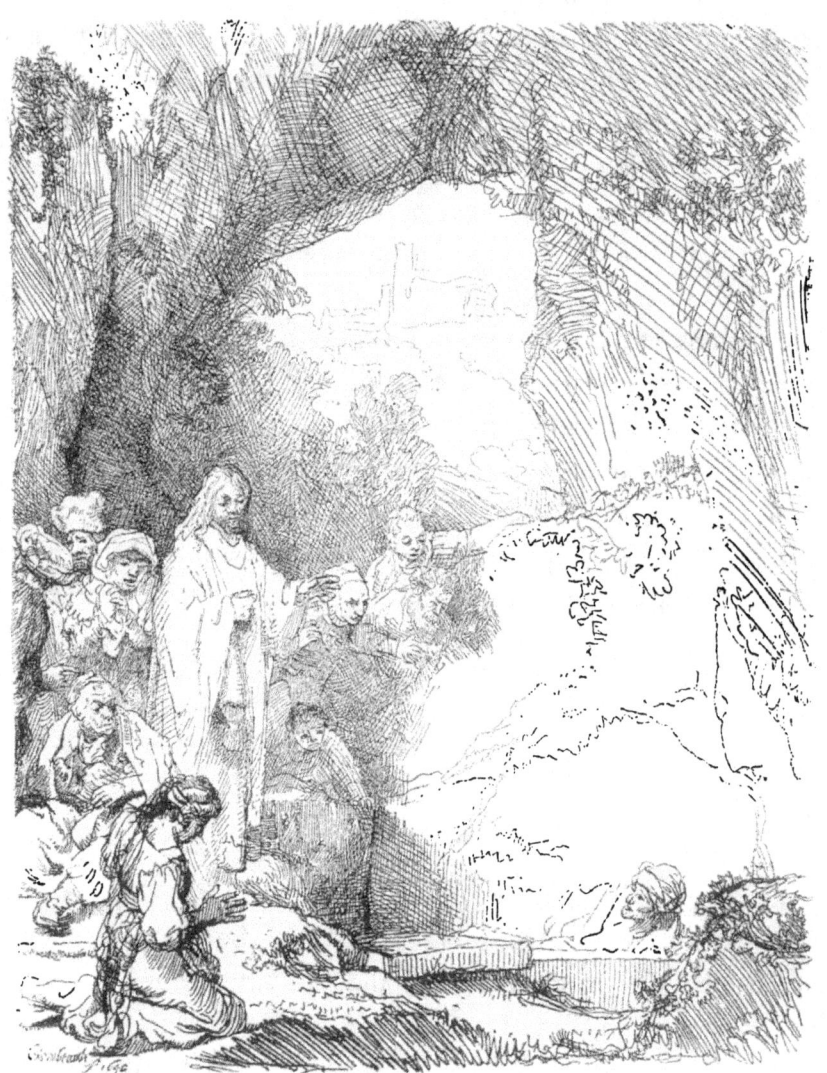

The Resurrection of Lazarus, A Small Print.   *B. 72. M. 215.*

M. 214.) of which I shall have more to say elsewhere, a very slight linear sketch *The Descent from the Cross* (B. 82. M. 216.) a study of

second girl Cornelya. Mr. Middleton says, "to this marriage were born four children, three of whom died in their earliest infancy, the fourth, Titus, alone survived." M. Dutuit uses almost the same expressions.

The Three Trees. B. 212. M. 309.

a picturesque cottage with a boarded fence entitled *A Cottage with White Pales* (B. 232. M. 308.) and *The Resurrection of Lazarus: a Small Print* (B. 72. M. 215.). The last is known in French catalogues as *La Petite Résurrection de Lazare*, and will be referred to later in comparison with the large etching of the same subject.

The year 1643 brings us to two good things—an excellent animal study *The Hog* (B. 157. M. 277.), in which the animal is represented lying down with its hind legs tied together, and a fine landscape well known to all lovers of Rembrandt as *The Three Trees* (B. 212. M. 309.). I happen to know by a positive test, that this plate is far more popular than one would have been likely to imagine. The best test of popularity is the separate sale of Amand-Durand's reproductions. He tells me that this plate sells better than any other.[1] It is a grand suggestion of landscape effect, but without any attempt (probably without any desire) to imitate the quality of clouds or the softness of falling rain.

I have only found one signed etching for 1644, a small plate called *The Shepherd and his Family* (B. 220. M. 310.).

It is unquestionable that after the death of Saskia Rembrandt was led much more than formerly to the study of landscape. He probably went out more, or his walks were more solitary, so he made sketches from nature, sometimes on paper, sometimes directly on the copper. For the year 1645 we have the *View of Omval, near Amsterdam* (B. 209. M. 311.), an important and masterly performance, and also the summary sketch of *Six's Bridge* (B. 208. M. 313.), a first-rate example of rapid selection in landscape by which all the parts of a scene, in their due relations, are described with a minimum of labour. The influence of this plate is visible in the slighter works of many modern artists, particularly in those of Jongkind. Two religious subjects of this year, *St. Peter* (B. 96. M. 219.), and *A Repose* (B. 58. M. 218.), are slightly sketched and very little bitten, that little being in one biting. Possibly Rembrandt may not have intended to leave the plates in this condition,

---

[1] Judging by his separate sales, M. Amand-Durand believes that *Christ Healing the Sick* (the Hundred Guilder Print) is the most popular of Rembrandt's etchings, but its sales are not so large as those of *The Three Trees*, because the price of it is six francs, whilst that of *The Three Trees* is only two. Still, it is very surprising that a landscape should come second, as many of the figure-subjects are sold for its price, or less.

but they are charming sketches, answering, in etching, to work done with
the silver point or a very hard, well-sharpened, lead pencil.

The reader will remember that mention was made of a portrait of.
J. C. Sylvius, etched in 1634. I ventured to say that I did not admire
it. I do, however, very heartily appreciate the merits of the etching of
1646. *Jan Cornelis Sylvius ; an oval Portrait* (B. 280. M. 155.) is one of
Rembrandt's finest works, as the other, if entirely by his hand, ought to
be frankly classed amongst his failures. Still, even this expressive and n os.
life-like portrait of the preacher is injured by the superfluous work round

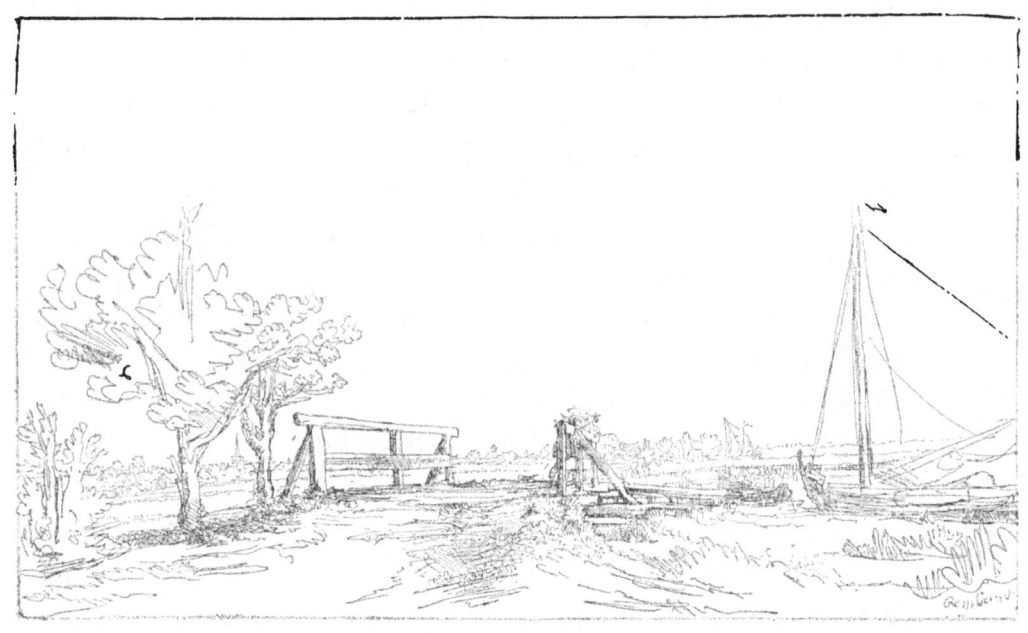

Six's Bridge.   B. 208. *M.* 313.

about it, by the rude oval frame, by the too numerous engraved words,
and also by the dull shading in the background which has so little artistic
quality that it may easily have been put in by an assistant. The face is
so strong and earnest in its eloquence that after looking at it for a minute
we feel ourselves to belong to the congregation. "He, being dead, yet
speaketh."

The year 1646 may be noted for some attempts in a kind of art for
which etching is not particularly well qualified, the representation of the
naked figure. Two studies of that year deserve especial attention, *An*

Academical Figure seated on the Ground (B. 196. M. 278), and *A Figure, formerly called " The Prodigal Son "* (B. 193. M. 279). It appears that the second is still called " The Prodigal Son " in Holland though it is obviously nothing more than an ordinary study of the nude. The model is seated on a stool or chair behind which is a dark curtain that puts his flesh into vigorous relief. He is etched strongly and simply as one might sketch with a pen, and without any idealisation of the forms. The other study has the same general characteristics but without such strong oppositions of light and shade. They are good straightforward sketch studies of very poor models, executed on the principles of the strictest realism. After saying this, I need not add that they are far from being beautiful, but they are honest and strong work.

Two etchings, only, bear the date of 1647, but these two are of capital importance. One is the noble portrait of *Ephraim Bonus* (B. 278. M. 158.) and the other the not less remarkable *Portrait of Jan Six* (B. 285. M. 159.). It was Rembrandt's habit to try over and over again for some quality that he desired but not to fatigue himself by toiling continuously for the same object. He always gave himself intervals, not of leisure, but of variety in his work, after which he tried again to do better what he had before attempted with more or less partial success. Almost every etcher has tried, at one period of his existence, to etch a plate in full tone. It is not necessary, as some of the finest etchings present only a selection of tones, but it seems to be an inevitable ambition, as every prose-writer has written verse and every engraver has tried to colour. These two etchings are both in full tone. Ephraim Bonus was a Jewish physician, he has been to see a patient, and is still, perhaps, reflecting on the case as he pauses with his hand on the banister of the stair. The plate looks like an etching from a picture, and there is, or was, in the Six collection a portrait of Bonus in the same attitude painted by Rembrandt, on the same scale as the etching.

The portrait of Jan Six is unquestionably Rembrandt's masterpiece in the way of highly-finished shading, and was evidently executed with the intention of carrying his art, for once, as far as was possible for him in that special direction. For a hand like his, accustomed to the utmost freedom, such success in patient labour may appear surprising, but it has an exact parallel in the high finish of some of Rembrandt's paintings. The interest of the plate is, however, by no means limited to its technical excellence. It is a charming, and was in its own day also a new and original, presentation of a cultivated gentleman in the privacy of his own room. Tranquillity and sobriety in everything are here the dominant notes. The subject appears quite unaware that he is watched, and reads, as he thinks, in solitude, near his window, and so it is one of the most unaffected of all portraits. I ought to add that the perfection of the technical work can only be appreciated by consulting a fine impression. The copper began to wear early and is now worthless for printing, however interesting as a relic or a curiosity.

Jan Six, afterwards Burgomaster, was already, when portrayed by Rembrandt, the author of a tragedy which gives its title to an etching of the following year, *Medea, or the Marriage of Jason and Creusa* (B. 112. M. 286.). It is rather a large plate but not otherwise worth especial notice. The year 1648 also gives us the most important of all the artist's beggar subjects, *Three Beggars at the Door of a House* (B. 176. M. 287.), a brilliant etching, in which the search for full tone is entirely abandoned, as there is no indication of local colour in the beggars, and it is suggested only in the dress of the almsgiver in his doorway. This plate is very nearly related to *The Rat Killer* (B. 121. M. 261.) which is almost the same composition and has the same absence of local colour. There is some relationship too between *The Three Beggars* and *The Three Oriental Figures* (B. 118. M. 212.) who are also at the door of a house. Judging by the sales of the Amand-Durand reproductions, the etching of the Beggars comes third in modern popularity amongst all the works of Rembrandt. A minor etching of the same year, *A Jew's Synagogue* (B. 126. M. 288.), remarkably full of human character and artistic effect, is executed precisely on the same principles. One of the numerous St. Jerome subjects also belongs to this year, that is *St. Jerome writing, seated near a Large Tree* (B. 103. M. 223.). Practical students will notice that Rembrandt first etched his subject, and then, not being satisfied, made some hurried and vigorous additions in pure dry point which do not at all harmonise with the rest. This etching is a good specimen of the mighty master's autograph, but the tree is so predominant that St. Jerome is little more than a landscape figurine. The most interesting plate of 1648 is a very fine and very serious portrait of the artist himself, *Rembrandt Drawing* (B. 22. M. 160.). The days are now gone by when he dressed up for his own amusement and drew himself as a study of costume. He has gone through sorrow, but what a firm, strong, resolute face it is! And he needs all his strength to face the evil that lies before him.

There is no dated etching for the year 1649. A small sketch on copper, *The Bull* (B. 253. M. 289.), was dated by Rembrandt, but the last figure is lost. Mr. Middleton supplies its place with a 9, Vosmaer with a 0, Dutuit avows his inability to make a guess. In reality it is quite impossible to fix dates from Rembrandt's ever-varying styles.

It would be very interesting to know the exact date of the famous "Hundred Guilder Print." Mr. Middleton assumes it to be 1649, Vosmaer places it more vaguely at some date "about 1650," so does Mr. Haden. M. Michel gives "about 1649." I myself venture no further than to say, from technical evidence in the use of line and shade, that the plate belongs to Rembrandt's ripe maturity.

Our certain dates for 1650 continue to illustrate the extreme variety of Rembrandt's methods of work and the range of his interest in things. One day he sketches, in his roughest and most rapid manner, *Jesus Christ in the Midst of his Disciples* (B. 89. M. 225.) and the next he sets himself to imitate, with the utmost patience, a beautiful sea-shell of a pattern presenting dark irregular reticulations. *The Shell, or Damier* (B. 159. M. 290.). This is sometimes also called *The Spotted Shell*, but inaccurately, as the pattern is a sort of dark network upon a light ground. The plate is of the greatest interest as Rembrandt's most decided attempt at pure and simple imitation, the model being chosen for its imitable character, and it is curious to see the great artist humbly giving himself this elementary lesson at the mature age of forty-three. At the same time he continues his practical studies of landscape and picturesque buildings, for example, in *The Three Cottages* (B. 217. M. 325.) and *A Village with a Square Tower* (B. 218. M. 321.). He also likes variety in the use of his tools, sometimes using etched, that is bitten, lines, and sometimes the dry point. Some of the etchings and sketches appear to afford evidence of travel. For example, there is a little landscape, otherwise unimportant, *Landscape with a Canal and Swans* (B. 235. M. 322.), which according to Vosmaer resembles the hilly scenery about Cassel, and the same authority saw in some picture or study a resemblance to the scenery of Oldenbourg. In another small etching of the year 1650, *Landscape with a Canal and Large Boat* (B. 236. M. 323.), the distance, though not mountainous, shows hills for which the artist must have wandered beyond the perfectly flat landscape of Holland. As to Rembrandt's studies in landscape, Vosmaer observes that although he began them early, his imagination did not take its flight until 1640 and reached the sublime about ten years later. However, he was always

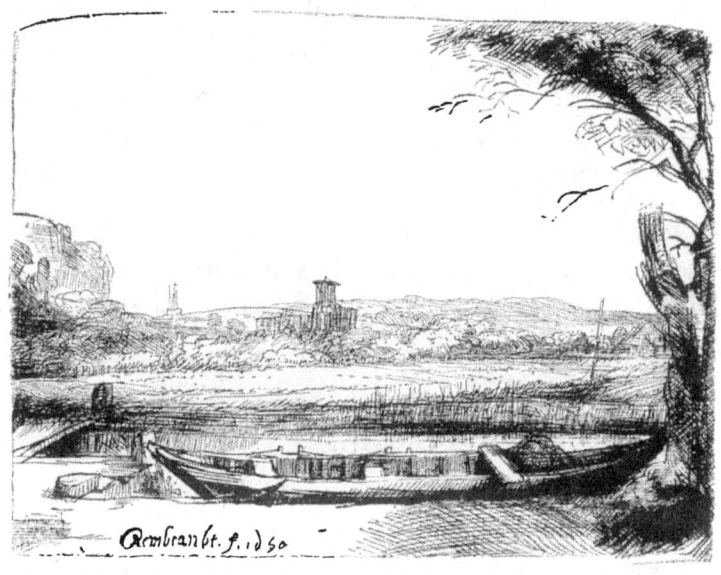

Landscape with a Canal and Large Boat. B. 236. M. 323.

changing, and in 1651 we find him making an important landscape etching, *The Goldweigher's Field* (B. 234. M. 326), which has every appearance of simple topography, the plain portraiture of a familiar place. So, in the human figure he makes, in the same year, a most prosaic little study of ugly nudities, *The Bathers* (B. 195. M. 292.), and one of his most touching Biblical illustrations, *Tobit Blind, with the Dog* (B. 42. M. 226.), a work in which the mental conception, which is most pathetic, is everything, and the manual performance so simple, so devoid of all pretension, that it requires some knowledge of etching to recognise the strength of a master. I much prefer the *Tobit Blind*, even as a piece of etching, to the black *Flight into Egypt: a Night Effect* (B. 53. M. 227.) which was etched in the same year. There is a strong resemblance, as to execution, between the *Tobit* and the dress of *Clement de Jonghe* (B. 272. M. 164.) also belonging to 1651, but the face of de Jonghe is carried much further and the quiet reflected light in the shadow

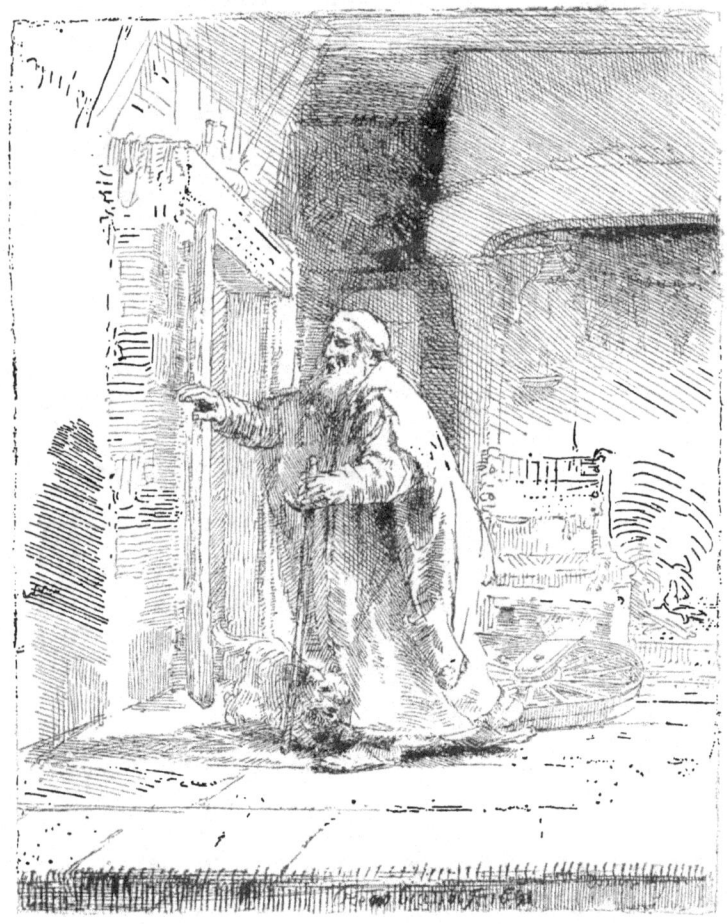

Tobit Blind, with the Dog. B. 42. M. 226.

of the hat is one of the best proofs of Rembrandt's complete mastery at this time.

The year 1652 offers rather a repetition of former successes than triumphs in any new variety of the art. The reader will understand that it was becoming rather difficult for Rembrandt, at the age of forty-five, and after at least twenty-four years of practice, to produce anything that was not visibly rooted in his own past. The *Jesus Disputing with the Doctors; the Larger Plate* (B. 65. M. 231.) is a masterly sketch like the *Tobit*, in which the imaginative conception of the scene far predominates over the simple handicraft. The *David on his Knees* (B. 41. M. 232.) has more " colour " but is near akin to the Tobit in pathetic intensity of sentiment. The reader may profitably compare it with official pictures of great personages going through prayer as a public function. King David is rather rudely drawn, and I will not undertake to defend

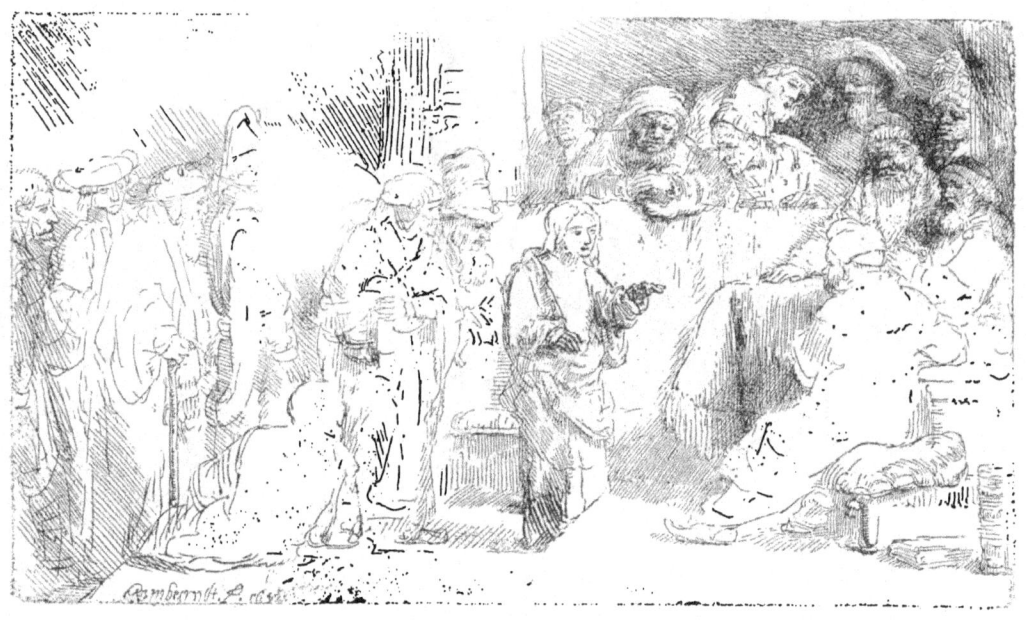

Jesus Disputing with the Doctors; the Larger Plate.   B. 65. M. 231.

the shading of his face, but he is thinking neither of crown nor harp, his whole soul is with the God of Israel. A landscape with this year's date is accurately called in the French catalogues, *Le Bouquet de Bois* (Charles Blanc, 323, Dutuit 219), by Mr. Haden, *A Landscape with a Vista*, whilst Mr. Middleton calls it *The Vista* (B. 222. M. 328.). The Italian word means either a prospect or an opening which gives the eye an escape into the distance (in French *une échappée*) and it is in this latter sense that the word is used in the English catalogues.[1]   The objection to

---

[1] The plate might be called in English *A Clump of Trees with an Opening to the Right.* If that is too long (it is not longer than many of the titles used for other etchings), *A*

Mr. Middleton's title is that the use of the Italian word by itself conveys the notion of a wider prospect, or of a landscape in which the distance is the chief thing.[1]   Here, the etching is blocked by a clump of trees with an issue round the corner to the right.   It is one of Rembrandt's finest works in pure dry point.   There is not a dry point in existence, by any master, that shows a more comprehensive and magisterial style.

VIII

The date 1653 is of sinister importance in the life of Rembrandt.   He then began to borrow money in large sums.   On the twenty-ninth of January he gets a loan of 4,180 florins from Cornelis Witsen, to be paid in a year. On the fourteenth of March, in the same year, he goes to Isaak van Hertsbeeck for 4,200 florins and also promises to pay in twelve months.   He is now rushing quickly down the slope, the end of which is ruin.

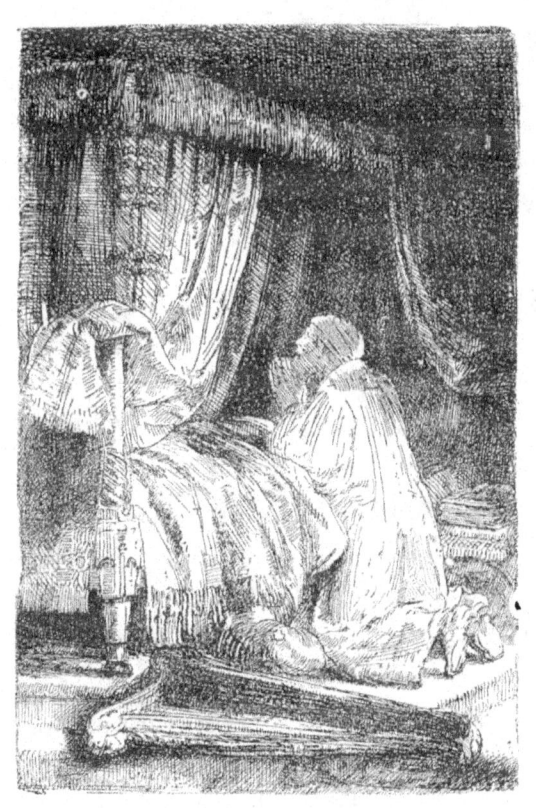

David on his Knees.   B. 41.   M. 232.

As in most instances of a like nature several different causes were operating together against him.   They will be enumerated later.

There is only one etching certainly of this year but it is of capital size and importance, *Christ Crucified between Two Thieves; otherwise known as The Three Crosses* (B. 78. M. 235.).   This magnificent

Wood Side would distinguish the work sufficiently and be more descriptive than *The Vista*, which one has to seek for.

   [1] An excellent example of a vista in the sense of *une échappée*, may be seen in *The Flight into Egypt, called 'In the Style of Elzheimer,' (B. 56. M. 236), where everything leads the eye to a lovely distance in an opening between the richest and densest masses of foliage, not a sneaking outlet on one side, like a servants' gate in a garden.

etching is in Rembrandt's broad and rapid manner, it is a linear sketch with masses of shading, the whole being far too quickly executed for any accuracy of form. We must take the work synthetically, as a whole, and not apply any detailed criticism. Rembrandt's sense of the grandeur of Christ has led him to give an exaggerated height to the body on the cross which, if we judge by the foreground figures, must at its own distance measure twelve or fourteen feet. The lighting is both supernatural and unnatural, but extremely effective. Our sense of its wonder and sublimity is perhaps diminished by our familiarity with the electric light, which gives similar effects of intense fan-shaped illumination whilst leaving outside things in darkness.

The Descent from the Cross: a Night Piece (B. 83. M. 242.) is called in the French catalogues the "Descent by Torchlight" which distinguishes it better from the great *Descent from the Cross*, where the lighting is supernatural. Both in conception and execution this is one of the most vigorous etchings of 1654. Its technical principles are the same as those of *The Three Crosses*, that is, organic lines with shade thrown over them, and with massive shade elsewhere in the plate. The idea is not so like that of a picturesque sculptor as the lofty group of the great *Descent from the Cross*, and this seems preferable in an etching.

The Flight into Egypt is one of Rembrandt's favourite subjects, and he treated it in the most various ways, at one time placing the Holy Family in a magnificent landscape, more Italian than Oriental, and at others in viewless nooks. *The Flight into Egypt, the Holy Family crossing a Rill* (B. 55. M. 240.) is of no particular locality, but we may suppose that the fugitive travellers have not yet escaped from Palestine and are crossing one of its brooks. This is one of the best of Rembrandt's small sketch plates in which an entire subject is indicated with little labour both in form and light and shade. The technical work, with a less display of power, is the same as that of the last plate we have been considering. The date is 1654. An excellent sketch plate of the same year, but in which line is somewhat more important and shade less, is *Jesus and his Parents returning from Jerusalem* (B. 60. M. 244.). The attitudes are most natural, the grandeur of the scenery seems to confirm the belief that Rembrandt must have travelled out of

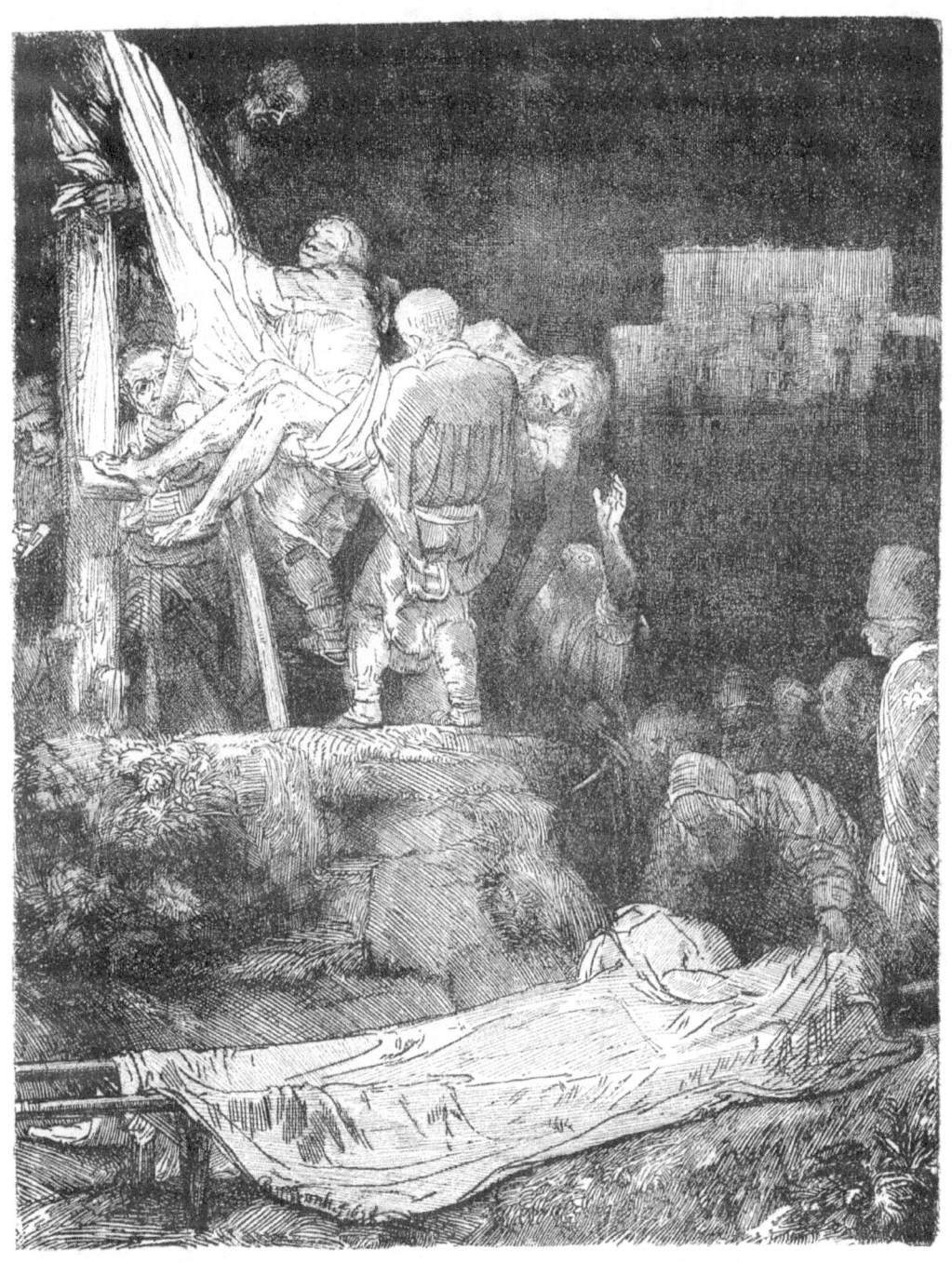

THE DESCENT FROM THE CROSS: A NIGHT PIECE.
B. 83. M. 242.

Holland.   Another of his favourite subjects was *Christ and the Disciples at Emmaus* (B. 87. M. 237.) of which we have a new version in 1654 It is a slight and rapid sketch, finely composed, but open to the obvious objection that if the disciples had prepared a stately seat under a canopy for their Master they must have known beforehand who He was, whereas St. Luke says He was revealed to them only after breaking bread. The nimbus is more defensible, for it may be explained as a sudden effulgence that astonishes even the innkeeper (or cook) who is descending

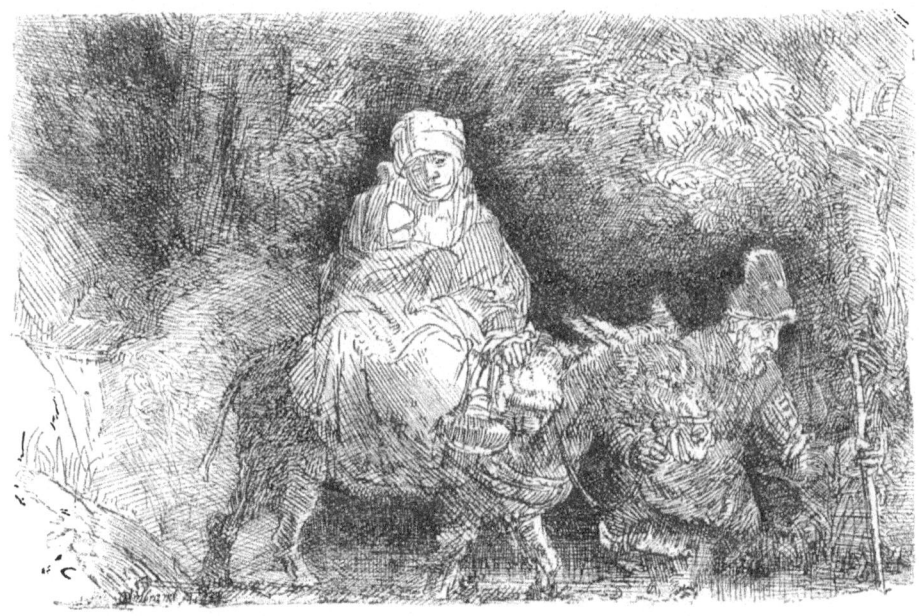

The Flight into Egypt, the Holy Family crossing a Rill.   B. 55. M. 240.

the stairs.   A still more striking interpretation of the same subject is a drawing by Rembrandt of which the reader will find an effective etching in Blanc's catalogue.   The figure of the Master is entirely absent from this composition; we see only the empty chair from which he has just vanished.

Jesus Disputing with the Doctors is one of the most interesting subjects for pictorial treatment in the New Testament, and we find Rembrandt recurring to it again in 1654 in a small plate (B. 64 M. 245.)   The attitudes, no doubt, are very natural, but I may be excused for preferring the conception of the boy Jesus in the larger plate, and also the placing of the other figures which seems to me more artistic.

IX

The close of the year 1654 is marked by another step on the downward path, for in the month of December Rembrandt appears before the sheriffs because he owes interest amounting to more than fifty-two florins

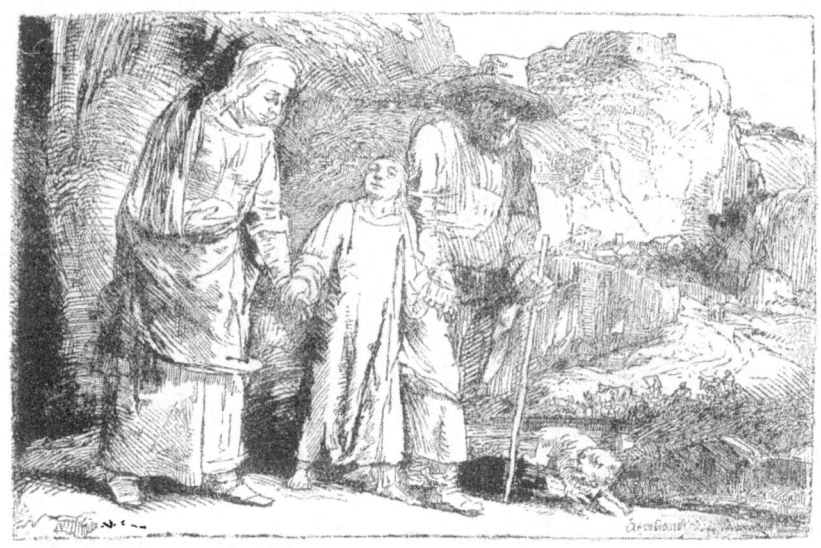

Jesus and his Parents returning from Jerusalem.   B. 60. M. 244.

on account of 1168 florins borrowed on mortgage, the security being his house in the Breedstraat. A portrait etched in 1655 has an interest connected with Rembrandt's affairs. It is that of *Thomas Jacobsz Haring* (B. 275. M. 169.) of whom, as a man of business, we shall hear more presently. The portrait is of a grave character, which is enhanced by a rich dark background resembling that of Jan Six, but of a coarser texture. Like the Six, it is obviously a study in darks. *Abraham's Sacrifice* (B. 35. M. 246.) is technically in the manner of *The Three Crosses* and *The Descent from the Cross by Torchlight*, and by its grandeur and originality of invention and composition may well take rank as one of Rembrandt's finest plates. *Christ before Pilate* (B. 76. M, 248.), which is more descriptively named in the French catalogues as *Jésus*

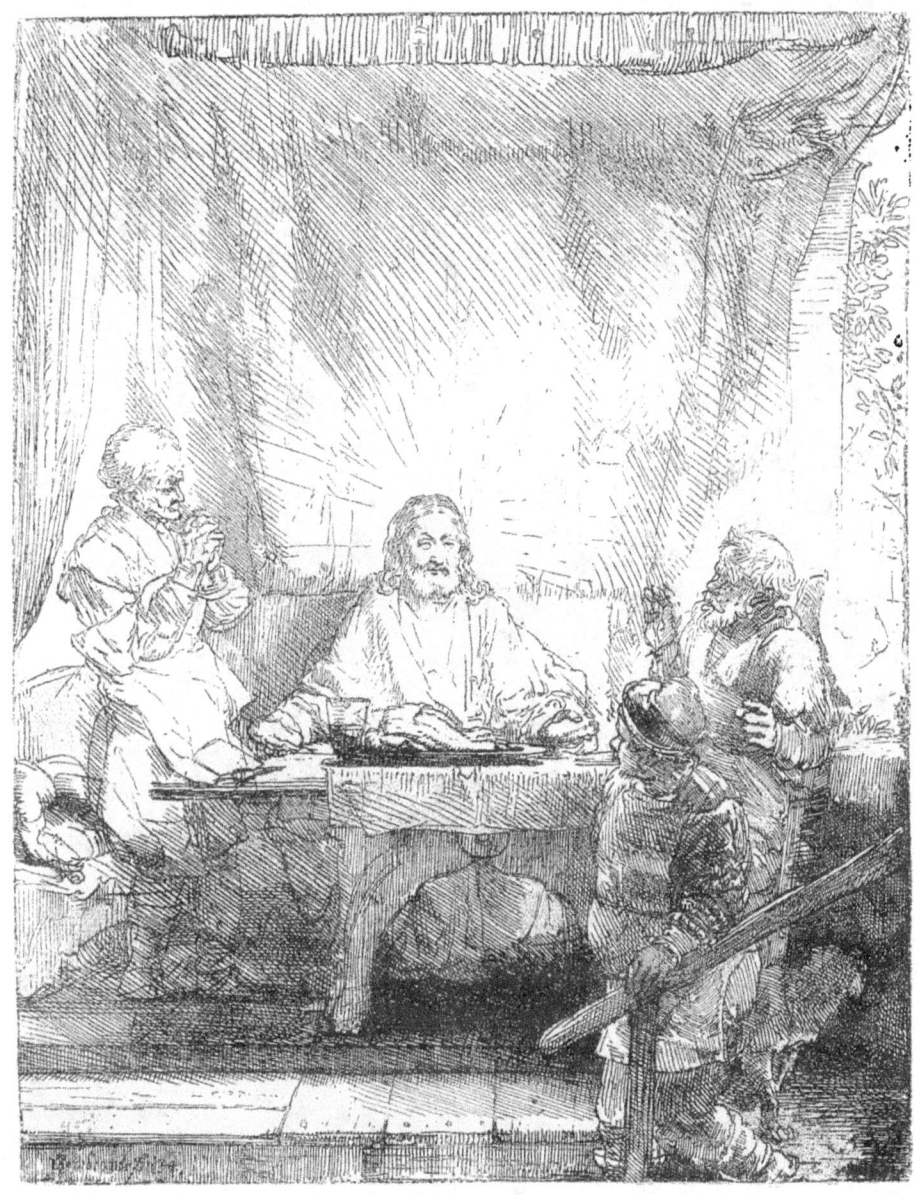

Christ and the Disciples at Emmaus. B. 87. M. 237.

Christ présenté au Peuple, is a very large plate, boldly sketched, representing a court in Pilate's palace where he shows Jesus to the people on a raised platform. There is some very grand and powerful linear sketching in this plate, having the characteristics of the etched line in all

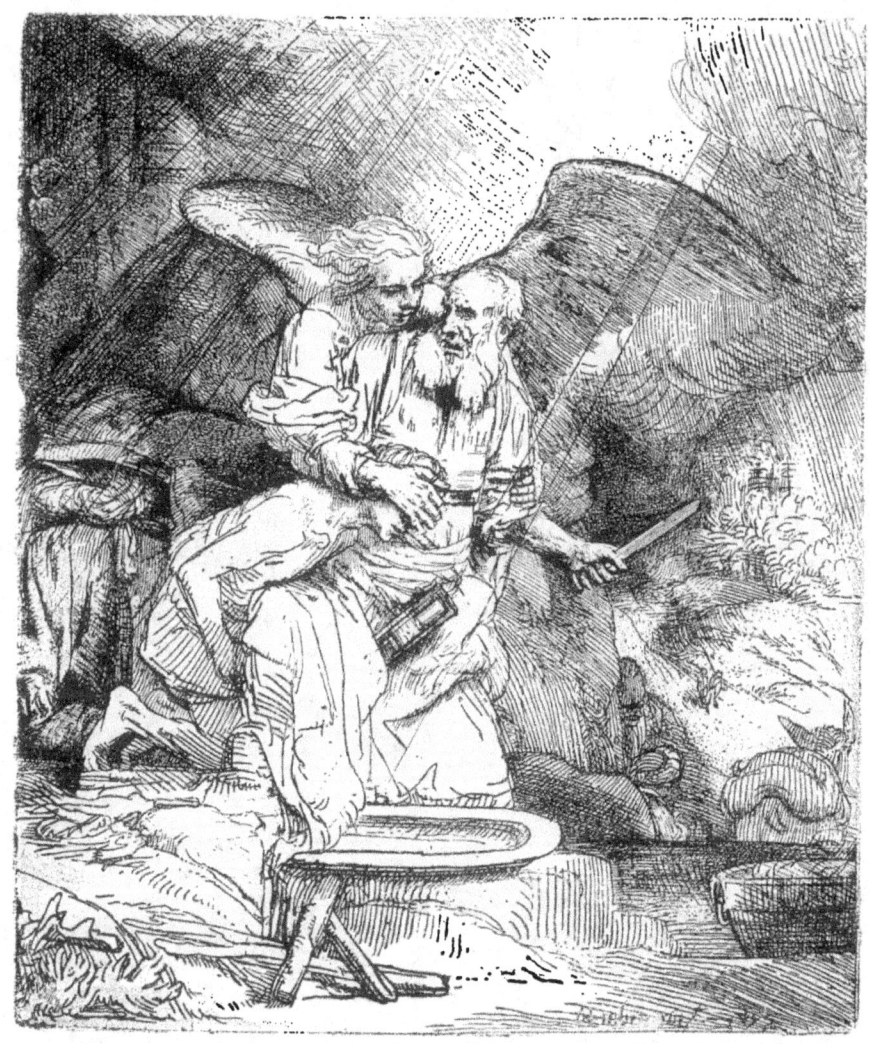

Abraham's Sacrifice. B. 35. M. 246.

its strength, but it seems certain that Rembrandt intended to shade a good deal over it, a process already begun in the building to the left.

X

In 1656 Rembrandt's affairs were in such a bad position that he transferred his house and land to his son Titus, then a minor of fifteen. However, with the consent of Saskia's relations, he is still to have charge of the property.

This was in the month of May, but the arrangement left the unfortunate artist little respite, for he was declared insolvent in July, all his possessions seized, and an inventory made of them by order of the Court of Bankruptcy.

These miseries do not prevent Rembrandt from etching one of his finest portraits, that of *Johannes Lutma* (B. 276. M. 171.), a most powerful and characteristic study, both of face and figure. The reader ought to see a fine impression of the *first* state.

Abraham entertaining Angels (B. 29. M. 250.) is in some respects an unfortunate attempt. The manual execution, for a sketch on copper, leaves nothing to be desired, but the conception of the scene is too matter-of-fact. For God and the Angels Rembrandt has given us simply Dutch burghers enjoying themselves at table, in a garden. It was Wilson who first observed that the old man with the wine-glass is not Abraham but God the Father, or according to some theologians, God the Son. The patriarch himself is humbly serving his guests and sits to the right, holding a ewer.

There is just one plate for 1657, *St. Francis Praying* (B. 107. M. 252.), of considerable importance as to size and of great technical interest. M Dutuit decidedly calls it one of Rembrandt's best works, and praises, as admirable, the patches of bur raised by the dry point. I see, of course, much manual power in this performance, and the figure of the saint expresses devotion well, but the plate is technically all out of tune. This may perhaps be attributed to the terrible trial through which Rembrandt was now passing.

XI

Thomas Jacobsz Haring, whose portrait Rembrandt had etched and whose grave face will thus be known to future generations so long as human beings continue to take any interest in the fine arts, was appointed by the Commissioners in bankruptcy to sell Rembrandt's goods. This first sale, however, which took place towards the end of 1657, did not include more than a part of the prints and drawings in the artist's collection. These were sold in September, 1658, at the same place, the Imperial Crown Hotel, kept by one Schuurman, who little knew the future value of what his house then temporarily contained. In February of the same year Rembrandt's mansion had been sold for 11,218 florins, its indescribably precious contents fetching about 5,000 florins, sums that went to his creditors and to the trustees of the interests of Titus, as his mother's heir, Rembrandt himself being left absolutely penniless at the age of fifty-one and severed from all the treasures of art in which he had taken delight.

Little remains to be said about the dated etchings. In 1658 the great etcher recurs to the interesting subject of *Jesus and the Samaritan Woman* (B. 70. M. 253.), a pleasant, harmonious plate with a distance reminding us (not in execution) of Dürer. There are also several studies of the nude, of no beauty, except a little perhaps in the recumbent figure of *A Negress lying on a Couch* (B. 205. M. 300.). In 1659 we have *Antiope and Jupiter* (B. 203. M. 301.), a composition that seems inspired by an Italian influence, probably that of Titian, whose genius the subject would have suited better. Even Rembrandt's etching is not without a suggestion of beauty distantly imagined, yet unattained. In the year 1661 he etched *The Woman with an Arrow* (B. 202. M. 302.), a naked figure seated on the edge of a bed, holding an arrow in her right hand, and turning her back to the spectator. This is one of those examples in which a work tells powerfully and effectively as a whole though it may be criticised in some part, even in a principal part. One might say, with truth, that the figure is still very inferior to the best Italian or even French drawing, yet the plate, as a whole, is fine because the figure is made to harmonise so perfectly with its well-invented surroundings.

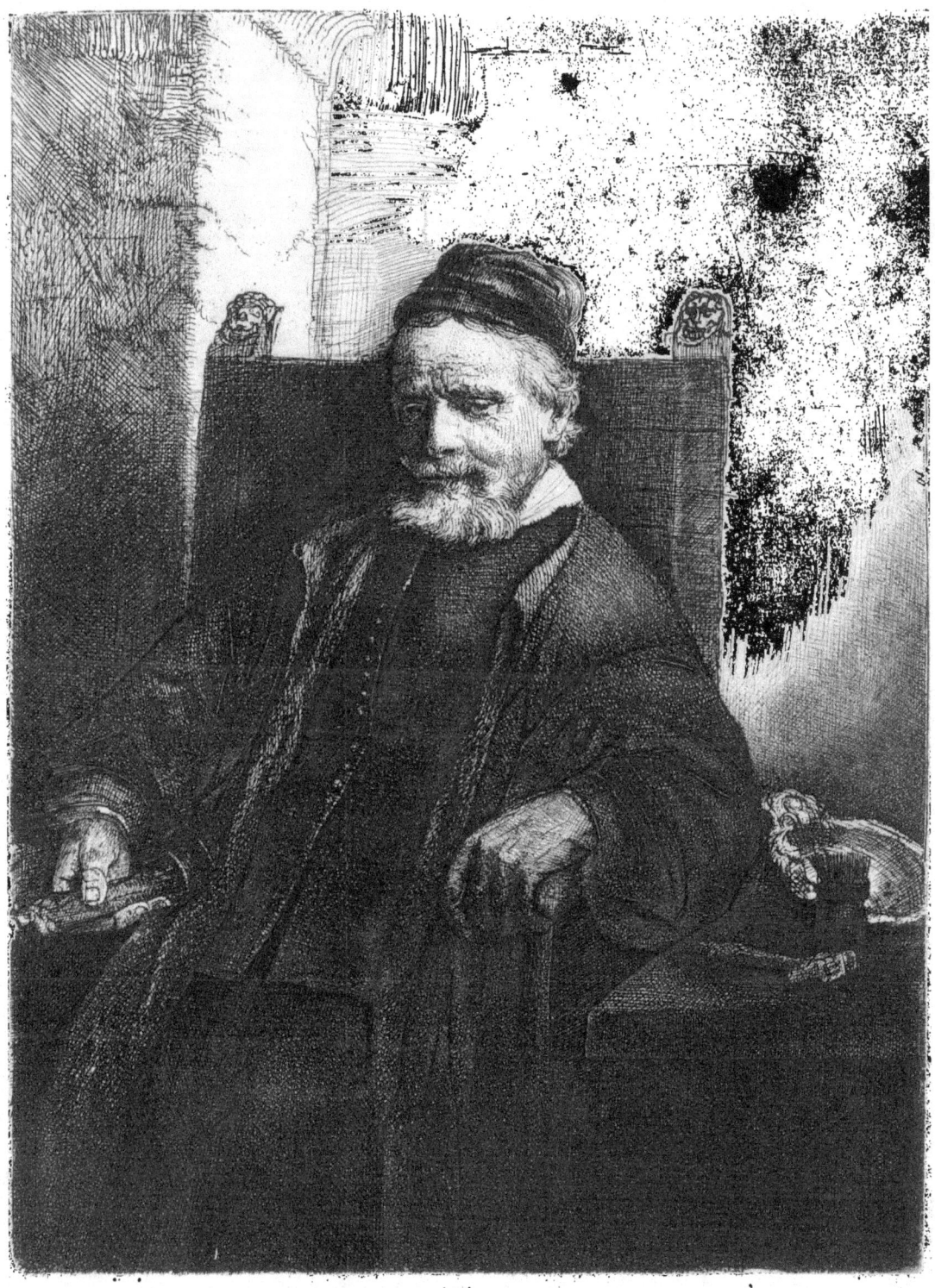

It is impossible to prove that Rembrandt etched anything after this, but he did not die till October 1669.

His son Titus had died thirteen months before him at the age of twenty-six, leaving a posthumous daughter, Titia. Her mother died less than three weeks after Rembrandt.

Vosmaer thought he had found satisfactory evidence that Rembrandt lived comfortably in his latter years, and in a good house on the Rozengracht, or Canal of Roses, which he says was not at all a poor quarter, only a little out of the way.[1] The ingenious Dutch biographer of Rembrandt also founds what appears to be a powerful argument on the merry looks of *The Laughing Portrait*, a picture that formerly belonged to M. Léopold Double, who kindly lent it to us for the

---

[1] The passage in Vosmaer's biography is so interesting that the reader may thank me for translating it.

"One day I went hunting about the Rozengracht to see if there were no traces of Rembrandt's last dwelling, no longer known. In front of what was formerly the site of the old *Doolhof*, on the north side, I noticed two fronts in an old style with shields dated 1652. Now, it was about 1656 that Rembrandt went to live on this quay On the ground-floor of one of these houses is the studio of M. Stracke, a sculptor. As soon as I entered and looked about me I was struck by a resemblance. Rembrandt had made a sketch of an entrance, probably in his own house. Through the doorway the drawing shows an entrance with two windows and an open door, and through these the foliage of a tree, a quay, and the fronts of houses across the canal. I found myself in the same place ! M. Stracke had the kindness to show me the whole house, and its present state made the past intelligible. The wooden floor that separated the cellars from the ground-floor is gone, but the brackets are still visible on which rested the ends of the beams. There are two rooms on the first floor ; that which looks out upon the quay once had a beautiful chimney-piece, and the walls are still covered with painted tiles, but they are now hidden under a modern wall-paper. Another room that may very well have served as a studio, is behind, and has three windows with a northern aspect. The owner told the present tenant that the building was formerly so rich in marbles that the value of them was equal to the price given for the whole house, even a pathway leading to some out-buildings was paved with marble, and still at the present day the kitchen floor is in marble from the quarries of Carrara !

"There is a drawing in the British Museum which was evidently made from the room with three windows in this house of the Rozengracht : it represents a studio, the three windows have small panes and look out upon a roof ; on a table before one of the windows is an object that may be a board or a portfolio.

" It is evident that in Rembrandt's time the house cannot have had the aspect of a poor place of refuge, where he had gone to live in destitution." Vosmaer's " *Rembrandt. sa Vie et ses Œuvres.*" Chap. XXXIX.

Portfolio. The reader will find the etching from it by Flameng in the *Portfolio* for January 1872. So far as we are able to ascertain, this is the last piece of self-portraiture that Rembrandt ever made, and the last we see of his honest face is jocund as the spring! Let us keep this cheering impression of the hard-working artist, the uncomplaining, practical philosopher!

Rembrandt was laid in his grave on the 8th of October 1669, at the age of sixty-two, having laboured incessantly at his vocation, as pupil, or master, about forty-nine years.

PART II

THE GENIUS AND CULTURE OF THE MASTER.

I

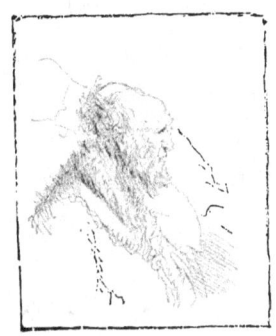

An Old Man with a Short Straight Beard. B. 306. M. 120.

THOUGH Rembrandt is a predecessor very difficult to approach in his own lines of work, it does not seem that his nature is hard to understand. It was a sound and simple nature with straightforward impulses and strong gifts. Amongst the supreme artists of the world no one had the graphic instinct and endowment more peculiarly and exclusively. Michael Angelo could turn aside from his painting and drawing to carve a statue or build a cathedral; Raphael, besides being painter and decorator, had the sense of construction so well developed as to be a competent, practical architect in the style of the Renaissance; Leonardo da Vinci was constructive, both as architect and engineer, besides having the acumen of a discoverer in science; Rubens had brilliant social and linguistic gifts, but Rembrandt was turned aside from his graphic occupations by none of these talents or tastes. He was, indeed, a lover of variety, he liked to refresh his intellect by change, but he found such variety as he needed in the graphic arts themselves, without seeking it outside of them. Though essentially a painter in oil colours, he was also a draughtsman in the most various materials, and he treated etching in such different ways as to divide it into five or six different arts.

Rembrandt was not entirely without literary instruction. He was sent, according to Orlers, to a Latin school with the intention of preparing him for the classical Academy of Leyden, "so that by his acquirements he might in due time serve the city and the Republic." We know from the same authority that Harmen's little son disliked his Latin studies, and may safely infer that his success in them was small. Still, the effect of this early schooling was not entirely negative, as in after life Rembrandt wrote letters in his own language of which Vosmaer gives a few in his biography, adding the remark that "any one at all versed in the epistolary style of that age in Holland, will see that these letters come from a cultivated man."

It is possible to have a sense of culture without much scholarly attainment, and the truest description of Rembrandt is to say that he was educated but not learned. He possessed a certain number of volumes, of which those specially mentioned in the inventory of his effects (when he became insolvent) are, with the exception of an old Bible, either books entirely made up of drawings or engravings or else, like his Josephus, illustrated. "Fifteen volumes of various sizes" are mentioned without separate designation, and it has been assumed that they were books to read, but some of them may have been purchased, like the rest, for their engravings. All this amounts to conclusive evidence that Rembrandt had not a scholarly or a literary turn of mind, for he lived in what was then, as it is still, an eminently learned little country. The evidence seems all the more convincing when we reflect that Rembrandt was an extravagant man and that he had the peculiar form of extravagance which does not consist in ostentation in style of living but in purchasing what one desires to possess. Such a man, if he had cared for books, would have collected a magnificent library. If, however, any reader feels inclined to accuse Rembrandt of Philistinism, let me say in his defence that he was not more Philistine with regard to literature than most people in our educated classes are with regard to art. If he bought only fifteen books, have we not many gentlemen and scholars who have *not* bought fifteen portfolios of original etchings or engravings? The essence of Philistinism lies in insensibility to the influences of genius and in unawakened observation. On these two points the evidence in Rembrandt's favour is overwhelming. His collections prove conclusively that he delighted in the works of other artists, for which he competed enthusiastically and beyond all prudence in the auction-room, whilst as to the observation of nature, his own works are still with us to testify like a multitude of living witnesses.

Rembrandt is the representative of the graphic intellect which notices, imitates, and remembers the forms of things, yet does not stop at the form but perceives that all shapes are significant. The scholarly intellect substitutes words for things and proper names for personalities, after which it deals with these substitutes as financiers deal with figures. The graphic intellect has its own processes of substitution of which Rembrandt's etchings afford many curious and interesting examples, but the visible forms of nature, though often noted in a sketcher's shorthand, are never lost sight of or forgotten.

"In the mind of such a man," said the elder Leslie, "the immense amount of knowledge accumulated by close and silent observation, knowledge of a kind not to be communicated by words, is something wholly inconceivable to the learned merely in books ; and if their reading has opened to them a world from which he is shut out, he also lives in a world of his own, equally interesting, the wisdom and enjoyment of which his pencil is constantly employed in communicating to all who have eyes for the sublime aspects of nature, and hearts fitted to receive such impressions through their eyes."

I believe that Rembrandt was as safely guided by his instincts in his abstinence from certain pursuits as in the zealous industry with which he addicted himself to others. The dictionary tells us that "the humanities," in the plural, are "the branches of polite or elegant learning, as language, grammar, rhetoric, poetry, and the study of the ancient classics." But surely if any works in the world belong essentially to the "humanities" they are the works of Rembrandt himself, for no one has ever shown a profounder or a more catholic interest in man. Both the limits of this essay, and its special subject, forbid me to range at will over all the fields of Rembrandt's art, but in the one field that is open to me I find ample proof of the most catholic human sympathies, and it may be for this reason that whilst we admire the skill or culture of some artists (as, for example, the stern self-discipline of Ingres imposes itself on our respect) we do not admire Rembrandt merely, but it seems to us that we have known him personally and that we keep the memory of him fresh and green in our affections. Let us remember, too, that his interest in humanity was unfeigned, that it did not express itself merely in pictures that he might hope to sell, but in hundreds of memoranda done evidently for himself and out of pure love of his subjects and pleasure in the constant practice of his art.   Even the etchings, which might legitimately have been a source of income, were unprofitable in the artist's life-time.   The famous *Hundred Guilder Print* is not believed to have brought Rembrandt that number of coined guilders, he only exchanged a proof of it for some engravings by Marcantonio which the dealer who offered them chose to value at that sum.   Vosmaer says that the time and trouble he gave to

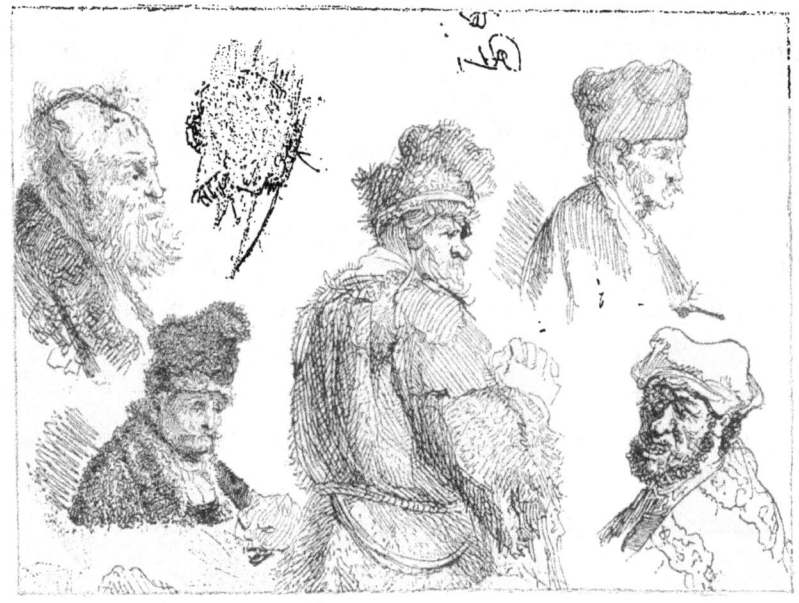

A Sheet of Sketches, afterwards divided into Five.   B. 366. M. 83.

his etched portraits were certainly not remunerated.   We cannot affirm that more than two of the etchings were sold by the trade, the others were kept for presents or exchanges, or disposed of occasionally by the artist.

It is clear, I think, from the etchings themselves that they cannot have been in any sense a mercantile speculation, with the exception of a very few plates, principally of large dimensions.   The great majority are simply an artist's expression of his own mind, many are simply memoranda, like *A Sheet of Sketches, afterwards divided into Five* (B. 366. M. 83.), all may be taken as faithful reflections, during at least thirty-three years, of Rembrandt's varying interests in human life, in landscape, and in the technical resources of etching itself. I propose to consider life and landscape in this Part and to reserve technical matters for the next.

II

The very earliest stage of human existence is generally more attractive to the feminine than to the masculine mind. It was not entirely neglected by Rembrandt, but he does not appear to have taken any very lively interest in infancy by itself, the charm of it, to him, was in its dependence upon parental love. If the reader is able to refer to a plate called *Academical Figures of Two Men* (B. 194. M. 280.) he will see in the background a slight and pale sketch of an entirely different subject, a child in a go-cart encouraged by an old woman. This little scene of infantine life is charmingly imagined, but Rembrandt valued it so little that he used the same plate for a commonplace study of the nude. Other works[1] prove that Rembrandt was not indifferent to babies, but it was the affection of parents that interested him most, an affection touchingly expressed in the attitude of the Virgin in *The Holy Family with the Serpent* (B. 63. M. 241.) where she is bending over the child so lovingly and laying her cheek to his. So in *Abraham caressing Isaac* (B. 33. M. 203.) the patriarch caresses the boy's face very tenderly and the boy is happy to be there between the paternal knees. Rembrandt had himself lost children in their infancy and could sympathise with all parental feeling, as when he etched *Jacob lamenting the supposed Death of Joseph* (B. 38. M. 189.) and the affecting plate of *The Virgin mourning the Death of Jesus* (B. 85. M. 202.).

The peasant children in Rembrandt's etchings are far from being attractive little creatures, and it is probably not a loss that we are unable to see those in the dark plate of *The Schoolmaster*. Nor is the child in

[1] There is a delightful little sketch of a sleeping child in the possession of Sir Frederick Leighton, reproduced in M. Michel's book on Rembrandt, and the reader will find in the same volume a family picture from the Brunswick Gallery, in which are three little children that appear both graceful and good-tempered. A very touching sketch, anticipating a well-known English picture, represents a widower gently trying to feed his baby, that appears to be unresponsive.

the *Three Peasants Travelling* (B. 131. M. 153.) a promising specimen of his race. It cannot be said that the etchings prove any delight in the beauty of young children. Even when we follow the models to maturity we do not often meet with any grace or elegance, quite a rare and exceptional instance being the figure of the young man in *Youth Surprised by Death*. The etchings in which Rembrandt attempted to represent the naked figure at its best time, for example the *Academical Figures of Two Men* (B. 194. M. 280.), are the most matter-of-fact interpretations without any sensitiveness to the beauty of the body or any evidence of the instinct which disengages a latent elegance that nature obscurely suggests. Closely connected with this indifference to the corporal beauty of youth, is the inability to conceive or express voluptuousness, of which there is never any trace in the works of Rembrandt. I am aware, of course, that three or four of his etchings represent certain actions that belong to the animal nature of man, but they are completely severed from everything that is seductive or poetical in form or motion. The plastic and graphic arts have often, like poetry, made it their business to idealise physical passion, and this may be done successfully by associating it with beauty of form and tenderness of sentiment.[1] There is nothing of this refinement in Rembrandt. He cannot approach a certain side of

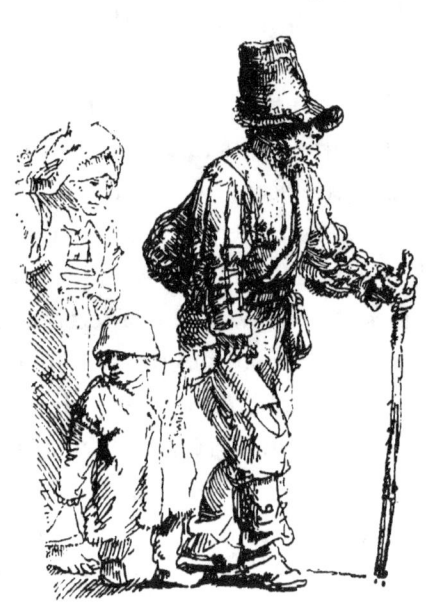

Three Peasants Travelling. B. 131. M. 153.

---

[1] The classical painter, David, a most severely-disciplined artist, once painted Cupid and Psyche so as to tell all that painting ought to tell of youth, and beauty, and love, and he did it with an art so delicate that it is impossible to reprove him. Shelley had the same delicacy, as for example in his Epithalamium and in his little Italian poem containing the stanza :—

> " Solinga, scura, cupa, senza speme,
>   La notte quando Lilla m'abbandona :
>   Pei cuori che si batton insieme
>   Ogni notte, senza dirla, sarà buona."

nature without grossness and therefore keeps habitually away from it as if warned by a consciousness of deficiency. There are, indeed, two deficiencies in Rembrandt with regard to this, his lack of ideality and the insufficiency of his classical culture.

It might be argued that Rembrandt drew the body with the same veracity as the hands and face, and that our criticism betrays a want of consistency in ourselves, since we approve of truth in the representation of the features and object to it in the trunk or limbs. Certainly Rembrandt never palliated plainness, he described even the ugliness of his own nose (B. 4. M. 42.), but whenever the human face is in question there may always be a ready and ample compensation for the lack of beauty in the presence of intellect and character, or, if these are wanting, in pathos. It is a sign of gentle feeling in a young man to take a respectful interest in age. Rembrandt began early in life to write on copper his own immortal treatise *de Senectute*. His strength lay in his respect for the wisdom of maturity and the dignity of declining years. His best portraits always represent either grave and learned men like Ephraim Bonus and Cornelius Sylvius, or old men like *Jacob Haring* (B. 274. M. 168.), one of his finest works. No author ever described more gently than Rembrandt has done in that portrait the slow approaches of senility. Some of the most interesting heads of old men

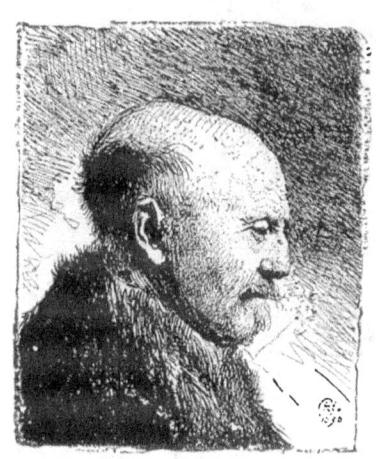

Profile of a Bald Man with a Jewelled Chain. B. 292. M. 39.

are without names, and all we know is that they once existed. Rembrandt seems to have taken an interest in them for the most various reasons. Their hair and beards, if luxuriant, were delightful to etch, but baldness interested the artist also, and we find several studies of bald men, like this one called a *Profile of a Bald Man with a Jewelled Chain* (B. 292. M. 39.).[1] He amused himself by noting the various stages and degrees

---

[1] It is the first state that shows the chain of the order, the second state is altered, and the third shows heavy additional work, which M. Dutuit supposes to have been added by another hand.

of baldness, for example, it is incipient in the little etching called by M. Dutuit *Téte à demi chauve* [1] (B. 296. M. 95.), whilst it is lamentably complete in another little etching, *Bust of a Bald Man, leaning forward to the Right with his Mouth open* (B. 298. M. 56.). We know from many pictures and etchings that Rembrandt fully appreciated a fine beard, yet he could turn aside to note the poverty of a thin stubbly one as well as cranial nudity in *An Old Man with a Short Straight Beard; a Profile to the Right* (B. 306. M. 120.), reproduced on p. 59.

Amongst all Rembrandt's numerous studies of old age, I know of none more observantly truthful than the delightful little etching of

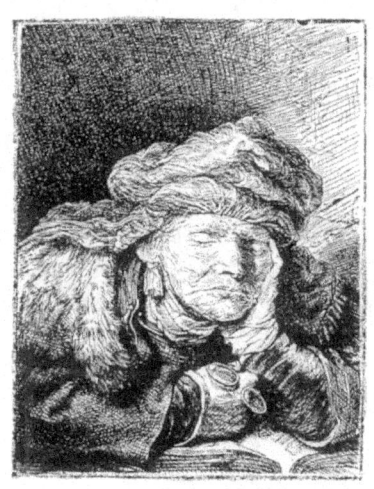

An Old Woman Sleeping. B. 350. M. 116.

An Old Woman Sleeping (B. 350. M. 116.). This seems to have been long a popular plate, as it has been often copied, once by Andrew Geddes. I do not know any work by the master that contains so much of his human sympathy and such abundant evidence of observation on so small a scale. The old lady, comfortably as well as picturesquely clothed, has been reading her Bible and has been surprised by a sudden need of sleep, her head resting on one hand, the spectacles, no longer wanted, on the other. As a study, the little etching could not have been carried further. It reminds me of Leslie's opinion that " the prevalent tone of Rembrandt's mind, as shown in his art, is serenity. Where the subject allows him, his natural disposition seems always tranquil, and though serious, yet the very reverse of gloomy. He is the painter of repose, as Rubens is the painter of action." Rembrandt sometimes attempted violent action, as in the three rapidly executed sketch plates of lion hunts,[2] and it seemed to be a usual coincidence in his sketching

---

[1] I give a French title for once, as it is much more accurate than Mr. Middleton's, " Head of a Bald Old Man, inclined to the Left." The man is not old, his hair is still dark, and he is scarcely bald, as it is only thinning at the top.

[2] The large one (B. 114. M. 272.) has been already mentioned. The two smaller ones are etched in the same violently vigorous style for composition and action only, form

that when the subject was connected with energetic action the handling was bold, quick, and decided, concerning itself as little about a multitude of minor truths as a war-horse thinks of the field-mice beneath its feet. The reader may accept *A Battle Piece* (B. 117. M. 275.) as an expression of a temper which sometimes, but rarely, manifested itself in the works of Rembrandt. What he felt to be most in harmony with his own nature was quiet thought or peaceful and deliberate occupation. I

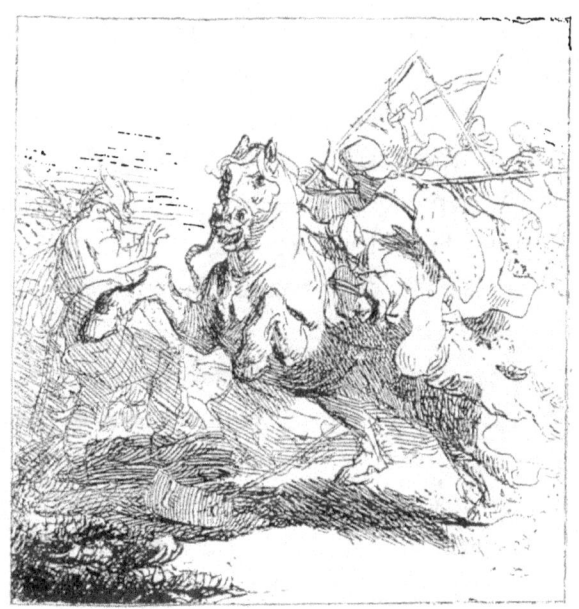

A Battle Piece. B. 117. M. 275.

should say, for instance, that the beautiful, lightly sketched *Old Man resting his Hands upon a Book* (B. 147. M. 156.) well represents the quiet thought, whilst the *Student in his Chamber* (B. 148. M. 276.) and *St Jerome; in Rembrandt's dark manner* (B. 105. M. 214.) represent the solitary work or study which the artist, though not himself a bookish man, could still appreciate and understand.

being of necessity sacrificed, as the shapes of letters are in the swiftest writing (B. 115 M. 273.) (B. 116. M 274.).

III

Some artists have an aristocratic turn by nature, as Rubens, Vandyke, Reynolds; others are naturally plebeian like Ostade, as in literature we have our genteel novelists who always introduce us to gentlefolks, and our plebeian or middle-class novelists who pride themselves on an intimate knowledge of the people. If it were asked to which category Rembrandt belonged, the right answer would be that he was too great to be either enviously hostile to the wealthy or contemptuous towards the poor. One of the imputations currently received against him was a taste for low society; the class he habitually lived in was that which follows the learned or the artistic professions; most of his friends were doctors, lawyers, clergymen, or painters and etchers like himself. He was not a tuft-hunter; he did not run after great folks. Having work enough in his art he sought only recreation in society, and expressed his taste in words that have become immortal. "Als ik mijn geest uitspanninge wil geven, dan is het niet eer die ik zoek, maar vrijheid." "When I wish to give rest to my mind, it is not honours that I seek, but liberty." A life divided between hard work and perfect ease left no room for that mysterious art of social advancement which has been for many a painter the secret of success.

IV

If Rembrandt was neither aristocratic nor democratic, ought we to say that he was religious? No one can deny that he was a most successful illustrator of the Old and New Testaments, not to mention the Apocrypha. Here he is a strong competitor with Raphael and Michael Angelo, though on principles the opposite of theirs. Whilst they endeavoured to idealise prophets and apostles, and to rise even to the representation of Divinity, Rembrandt had a clear vision of all religious personages as human beings. One of his compositions is called the "Ecce Homo." In a certain sense the title is applicable to them all. Even God the Father, in *Abraham entertaining the Angels*, is represented as an amiable human friend who appreciates a glass of wine. Christ, in the Hundred Guilder and many another print, is the Son of Man who sympathises with suffering in others or endures it patiently himself. When Christ is preaching, as in the etching known as *La Tombe* (B. 67. M. 229.), Rembrandt no more despises the humble listeners than did

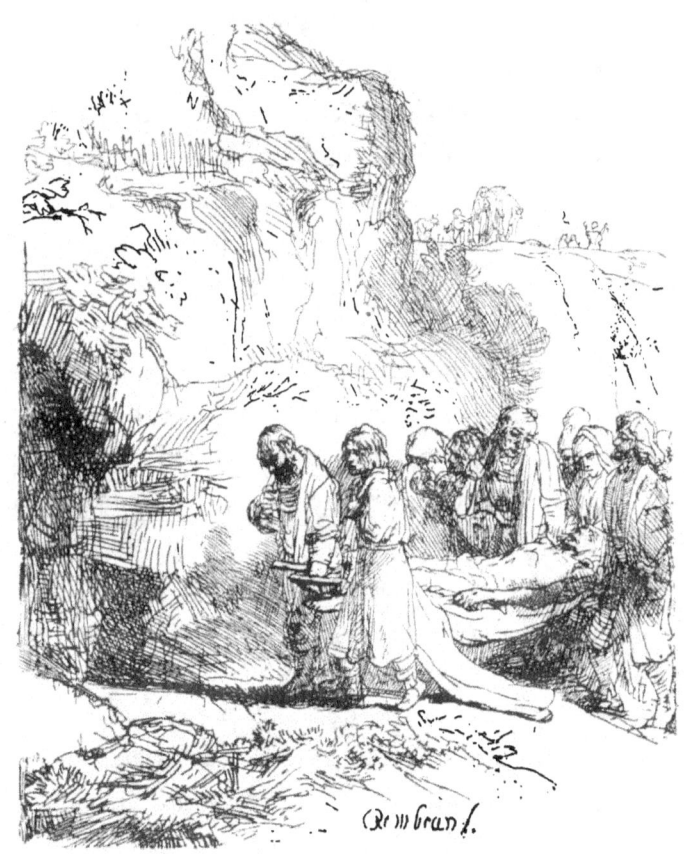

Christ's Body carried to the Tomb. B. 84. M. 217.

the Teacher who addressed them. When the voice is silenced, a pathetic little group bears the body, tortured no longer, to its quiet resting-place. This scene is represented in a little etching, *Christ's Body carried to the Tomb* (B. 84. M. 217.), in which the simple-hearted, affectionate followers are unconscious that theirs is the grandest funeral procession of all time.

V

In judging Rembrandt as a etcher of landscape we ought to bear in mind two considerations, first, that landscape was quite a secondary pursuit for him ; and, next, that he was situated in a country where the grander manifestations of natural glory in landscape are unknown. It is supposed that he may have visited some hilly, but not mountainous, district in Germany, and it has been affirmed, on very insufficient evidence, that he knew the neighbourhood of Hull. However this may be, Rembrandt had not a tithe of the landscape experience of Titian, nor a hundredth part of the opportunities of Turner. He knew nothing of Scotland, France, Switzerland, or Italy. He was deprived of at least half the materials accessible to him by his complete indifference to, and corresponding ignorance of, the sea. Neither had he Claude's exquisite sense of the richness of inland landscape. Add to this the peculiar limitations of the art of etching which are not favourable to those delicate distinctions of tone on which all the most impressive effects of distant landscape must depend. The consequences are, first, confinement to simple and homely subjects, and, secondly, great simplicity in the treatment of those subjects.

And yet, notwithstanding these limitations, we all look upon Rembrandt as a master, even of landscape. The reason for this may be expressed in a single phrase, his powerful expression of character. If he does not attempt to imitate the exact forms of a scene, or the tones of an effect, he shows you the nature of the place at the first glance and makes you feel as if you were there. No delineation of landscape was ever more penetrating or more comprehensive. Take, for instance, the *Landscape with a Ruined Tower and a Clear Foreground* (B. 223. M. 317.) and see how everything about the place is either explained or suggested. We have the rural village with its old church, and houses, and haystacks, and its gloomy wood, and the road that passes by. At the same time we are made to feel that it is in the open country, and an effect of stormy weather is suggested in dark distance and threatening sky, without any attempt at imitation. Nothing more, in the way of impression, could be communicated without colour. Essentially the same landscape in principle is the one called by Mr. Middleton *An Arched Landscape with a Flock of Sheep* (B. 224. M. 319).[1]

Here, too, we have an open foreground, the chief interest of the subject, as before, being in a mass of trees and a hay barn that occupy the middle distance, leaving an outlet to the left. I recommend the student to familiarise himself with the workmanship of this plate, because so many small landscape etchings have been attributed to Rembrandt that it is well to have in the memory a good type of his landscape executed on a small scale. For the same reason I mention *A Village with a Square Tower; an Arched Plate* (B. 218. M. 321.) and the *Landscape with an Obelisk* (B. 227. M. 324). There is also a small landscape that may be easily overlooked, but which has its own importance, *An Orchard with a Barn* (B. 230. M. 316.) These plates, notwithstanding their limited dimensions, are executed in as strong and simple a style as, for example, the *Landscape with a Ruined Tower and a Clear Foreground* (B. 223. M. 317.), whereas many little plates attributed to Rembrandt are weak and rather pretty, or not pretty at all but still weak, both in conception and in style.

On looking back over the landscapes I observe the following chief characteristics. First, a strong sense of the picturesque in foreground material as in the *Village with a River and a Sailing Vessel* (B. 228. M. 314.), next, in several plates, a disposition to throw the interest into the middle distance and sacrifice the foreground (see *Landscape with Ruined Tower, &c.*); lastly, a lively sense of the charm of a remote distance, as in the lovely outlook to the left in *A Large Landscape with a Dutch Hay Barn* (B. 225. M. 306.) and other instances. It is surprising that after the magnificent note of transient effect in *The Three Trees*, where the grandeur and motion of a sky are perfectly suggested, Rembrandt should not have attempted to etch other skies, but that remains alone with the single exception of the threatening weather in the sublime plate of *The Ruined Tower*. The inference is that Rembrandt was by no means indifferent to the impressiveness of skies in nature, but

---

[1] The French critics entitle the same plate *La Grange à Foin* or *La Grange à Foin et le Troupeau;* Mr. Middleton's title seems to attract too much attention to the sheep which do not strike the eye at the first glance. His word "arched" helps to distinguish the plate well.

was dissatisfied with their rudely linear interpretation in etching, as he practised the art.   His knowledge of water appears to have been extremely limited, a mere nothing in comparison with that attained by modern landscape-painters.   Rembrandt sometimes indicated the presence of water, but that was all; he never attempted to etch a wave, his study of reflections was rudimentary, the best instance being *A Cottage with White Pales* (B. 232. M. 308.).   He was strongest in picturesque buildings and next to that in trees, though his merit as an etcher of trees lies principally in his fine sense of mass, for he does not seem to have had any extensive knowledge of species.   Altogether, Rembrandt was a landscape etcher of great power, because he was such a forcible artist before he approached landscape, but, though he proved this in a few superb plates, his acquaintance with nature was most limited.   He has, however, exercised a great technical influence on landscape etching and through it on modern pen-drawing and landscape illustration generally. Besides, it would be unfair to judge of Rembrandt's studies in landscape from his work on copper alone, as there exist many sketches by him in other materials.

VI

Rembrandt took but little interest in animals, which occur very rarely in his etchings, and the most finished of these representations, *The Little Dog Sleeping* (B. 158. M. 267.), is probably by another hand.   There is another *Sketch of a Dog* (B. 371. M. 266.) in the corner of a plate of which the rest was left vacant; it is good, and evidently authentic. For the heraldic lion in *St. Jerome Sitting at the Foot of a Tree* (B. 100. M. 190.) I do not hold Rembrandt responsible, nor for the ass in *The Flight into Egypt; a Small Spright Print* (B. 52. M. 184.).   He is, however, answerable for the wild beasts in the large and lesser

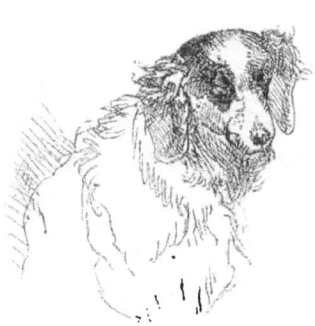

Sketch of a Dog. B. 371. M. 266.

Lion Hunts, which have energetic motion but are poor in size and shape (compare these wild-cats with the bronzes of Barye), and for the ass in

A Village with a River and a Sailing Vessel.   B. 228.   M. 314.

The Flight into Egypt; the Holy Family crossing a Rill (B. 55. M. 240.), which has the genuine asinine character and action.[1] This does not amount to evidence that Rembrandt had the love of domesticated animals that distinguished Paul Potter. Where, in the etchings, are his sheep? Where are his cattle or farm-horses, either in harness or at liberty in the fields? For an artist with Rembrandt's power of drawing, his attention to animal life seems strangely rare and languid in its interest, as it is impossible that he can have been turned aside from it by any consciousness of technical inability.

VII

The artistic personality we have been studying is one of great range and mighty energy, yet far from being universal. It is marked by a strong preference of maturity to youth and by an unfailing interest in age. Full of the most intense and pathetic human sympathy, even its religion is a " religion of humanity." It is indifferent to the division of mankind into patrician and plebeian classes, but not indifferent to the signs of culture and of thought. Its sense of beauty is picturesque rather than plastic, and attaches itself to effect rather than to form. It strongly prefers costume to nudity. It seeks refreshment and consolation in homely landscape, yet has some appreciation of grander and more romantic scenery. It pays a slight occasional attention to animals. With remarkable and rare powers of memory, invention, and manual execution, it is without any sure guidance in a cultivated taste, and remains therefore at all times liable to such errors as the *Adam and Eve* or the *Woman sitting upon a Hillock* (B. 198. M. 256.), whilst the only attempt at decorative monumental arrangement, *An Allegorical Piece* (B. 110. M. 296.), is top-heavy, straggling, and out of all reasonable proportions.

[1] I am not forgetting some studies of animals (particularly a lion and an elephant) outside of Rembrandt's etched work, to which, at present, I am obliged as much as possible to confine my attention.

PART III

TECHNICAL NOTES

I

THE reader is already aware that modern criticism does not admit the whole of the etched work formerly attributed to Rembrandt as genuine.

The result of certain inquiries has been, briefly, this, that we cannot any longer accept with blind confidence any work whatever that is attributed to Rembrandt, with signature or without signature, dated or undated.

We find ourselves, therefore, in a situation from which there is no logical issue, as we can only test the spurious plates by a comparison with the genuine ones, but, to know which *are* the genuine ones, we must have already distinguished them from the spurious, so that, in order to make the selection, we, in fact, must have already made it.

The biographical test, in Rembrandt's case, is hardly available, as there is so little documentary evidence. There was no zealous contemporary to make an accurate catalogue in the artist's life-time, as Sir Francis Drake did for the etched work of Mr. Haden. We have a few facts or traditions. There is, for example, *The Hundred Guilder Print*, which Rembrandt exchanged for some Marcantonios, but if it pleased me to affirm that the linear work only was by the hand of Rembrandt and the shading by an assistant, I might have the opinion of artists and connoisseurs against me, yet they could not effectually defend themselves. I should answer that down to a recent date all expert opinion accepted plates that we now reject, and I should quote their prices. A print of *The Descent from the Cross* has fetched £36, a

Raising of Lazarus £72, a *Good Samaritan* the same. An *Ecce Homo* has fetched £190 and a *Gold Weigher* £260, all of them prices considerably exceeding the poor £8 15s. which Rembrandt is said to have got for the Hundred Guilder Print (but did not). I may remind the reader that Bartsch admitted 375 plates into his Rembrandt catalogue whilst Mr. Middleton admitted only 329, and in a certain number of those admitted even by Mr. Middleton there is a great quantity of manual work that is not now believed to be by the hand of Rembrandt.

Mr. Haden and I may be asked why we did not discover the spurious plates twenty years sooner. Mr. Haden's answer is that he never admitted one of them into his private collection, or had the slightest desire to possess them; mine is that the plates selected for description in " Etching and Etchers " are all still admitted to be perfectly genuine. I well remember my feelings about the doubtful plates. I naturally trusted to the authority of the artists and connoisseurs of all nations who had accepted them, and as Rembrandt had adopted many different styles, I did not, at that time, see any reason why he should not have adopted at times what may be called an engraver's rather than an etcher's manner when it pleased him to reproduce designs already executed in some other medium. In a word I believed (and there were fairly good reasons for this belief) that Rembrandt occasionally executed for commercial purposes, what may be called industrial work in etching. It has since been suggested by Mr. Haden for reasons which to me are satisfactory and convincing, but which do not amount to positive proofs, that the industrial work formerly attributed to Rembrandt was, in reality, done for him by pupils or assistants, who, according to the practice of those days, and even the laws and regulations of their profession, were not permitted to sign their names. We are, indeed, compelled to choose between the two alternatives. Either, in certain plates, plates of which the conception and composition belonged to Rembrandt, the handicraft was done by himself purely as a matter of business, as we used to believe, or else it must have been done as a matter of business by anonymous pupils or assistants. It seems to me, now, that the latter is more likely—much more likely, considering the strong personality of Rembrandt's nature,—to be true, but our former belief is excusable for a peculiar reason. The case bears no resemblance to

ordinary cases.   Rembrandt was not like a Ruysdael, a Paul Potter, a
Turner, a Méryon, or a Samuel Palmer, who, each in his own way, had
a settled style in etching.   Rembrandt had at least half-a-dozen styles,
and these did not succeed each other in any steady chronological order,
but were resumed or thrown aside according to the whim of the moment.
For example, in 1647, he etches the famous *Portrait of Jan Six* (B. 285.
M. 159), which is the *ne plus ultra* of his finish as to tone and texture,
but in the following year his style becomes linear again, as in the *St.
Jerome writing, seated near a large Tree* (B. 103. M. 223.), or it
combines line and shade, without any delicacy of tone or quality of
darks, as in the *Marriage of Jason and Creusa* (B. 286. M. 112.).
Instead of persevering in a style when he had succeeded in it, Rembrandt
more frequently abandoned it for something else.   It requires, then,
considerable assurance in a critic to affirm of a changeable artist who
works in six styles that he has not, on another occasion, tried a seventh.
The most likely test is this.   We know enough of Rembrandt to perceive that he must have been a highly intelligent man.   If, therefore, any
workmanship attributed to him is manifestly mechanical, it is probably
due to some assistant.   We also know that Rembrandt was immensely
productive, and that he must have been a good economist of time.   If,
therefore, the mechanical execution had to be long and laborious (particularly in large plates) we may conclude that he would pass it on to
another, unless, as in the case of the portrait of Six, there was some
technical object in view which could not be attained by another hand.
As for the morality of signing work not literally, as to handicraft, one's
own, the old masters had no more scruples on that point in the graphic
arts than our own contemporaries have in the practice of sculpture.

The questionable plates attributed to Rembrandt are not, however,
confined to works of which the design is due to him whilst the manual
labour was supplied by assistants.   A considerable number of plates,
particularly but not exclusively landscapes, formerly attributed to
Rembrandt are now believed not only to have been executed by inferior
hands but conceived and composed by men of inferior artistic endow-
ments.   The reader perceives how much more serious is this question
than the other, as that related to handicraft alone and not to the first
conception of a work of art or the interpretation of nature.

II.

The reader may perhaps be surprised to hear that the supremacy of Rembrandt in etching is not founded upon any unapproachable technical superiority. It is mental, and manual so far as it proves the possession of great executive power, but in such matters as the use of different qualities of shade, thicknesses of line, and depths of biting, the cleverest professional etchers of the present day are Rembrandt's superiors, and it is probable that if he could examine their performances he would acknowledge it. We have clear evidence that his grounds were not always well composed or skilfully applied, that the bitings were certainly often deeper and occasionally shallower than he intended them to be, and that his chemical and technical science in all ways was less ad-

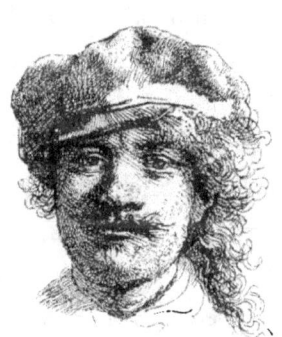

Rembrandt with Moustache and Small Beard. B. 2. M. 106.

vanced than our own is to-day. M. Amand-Durand, who has given a thousand proofs of the certainty of his own chemical operations, is persuaded that Rembrandt must have had what we should consider inferior resources at his disposal, that he must have been *mal outillé*. Such etchings as *Rembrandt in a Fur Cap and Dark Dress* (B. 6. M. 17.), *Rembrandt with Bushy Hair* (B. 25. M. 49.), and *Rembrandt with Bushy Hair, and strongly shaded* (B. 34. M. 43.), are good examples of involuntary face-blackening by too much acid, yet the hand that mismanaged these has given us the delightful little *Rembrandt with Moustache and small Beard* (B. 2. M. 106.), which, both for the perfectly intelligent management of the point and the precisely sufficient biting, is one of the most faultless works of art in the world.[1]

It is probably as a result of the bad quality of an etching-ground that Rembrandt's own great plate of *The Descent form the Cross* (B. 81. M.

[1] This plate has long been known by the ridiculous and almost unintelligible title *Rembrandt aux Trois Moustaches*. Even the "small beard" is objectionable, as it conveys an inexact idea. As we use the French word *moustache*, why not use the other convenient French word, *barbiche*, or, when a mere tuft, *impériale?*

186.) was destroyed in the biting.   As the labour with the needle had
been enormous, the artist does not appear to have summoned courage
to begin the weary task over again, so he entrusted a replica to other
hands, and it is from this copy that the current edition has been printed,
the spoiled plate having only yielded trial proofs enough to demonstrate
its worthlessness.   This failure shows the importance of good biting, as
the work with the point was much more artistic in the rejected plate than
in the well-bitten one that Rembrandt too carelessly allowed to go forth
under his own name.   Amongst minor failures from the same cause may
be mentioned *The Rat Killer ; an injured Plate* (B. 122. M. 260.).

A technical merit that Rembrandt often displayed in an exceptional
degree was his masterly way of combining strong and delicate work
in the same plate, of which there is an excellent example in *Rembrandt's
Mother, seated, looking to the Right* (B. 343. M. 54.), where the face
and hands are treated in one style of execution, the dress in another, and
the table-cover and background more summarily in a third   The
etching-needle thus becomes like three different instruments which
may be compared to musical instruments played together in concerted
music.   Such execution gives the pleasure of difference in unity.   It
strongly contrasts, for example, with the unintelligent uniformity of
Van Vliet's execution, which was excessively industrious, but only
resulted in opacity.

The intentional combination of different ways of handling the
point in a single plate is not to be confounded with an involuntary
mixture of styles, a fault to which the inexperienced are often exposed
because they have not the power of will and foresight that predetermines
the exact nature of a work of art from the first stroke to the last.
Nothing can prove more convincingly the vigour and sanity of
Rembrandt's intellect than the decision with which the executive scheme
or project of each work is settled before it is begun.   Each separate
etching is an enterprise in itself and may be a new experiment.   The
artist has all his powers and faculties under control, he is never carried
beyond his first intention by the seductive detail of nature, and he is
never prevented from observing nature by any fixed habit of execution.
Even in his full maturity he can cast aside styles in which he has been
perfectly successful, either to resume the practice of an old one or

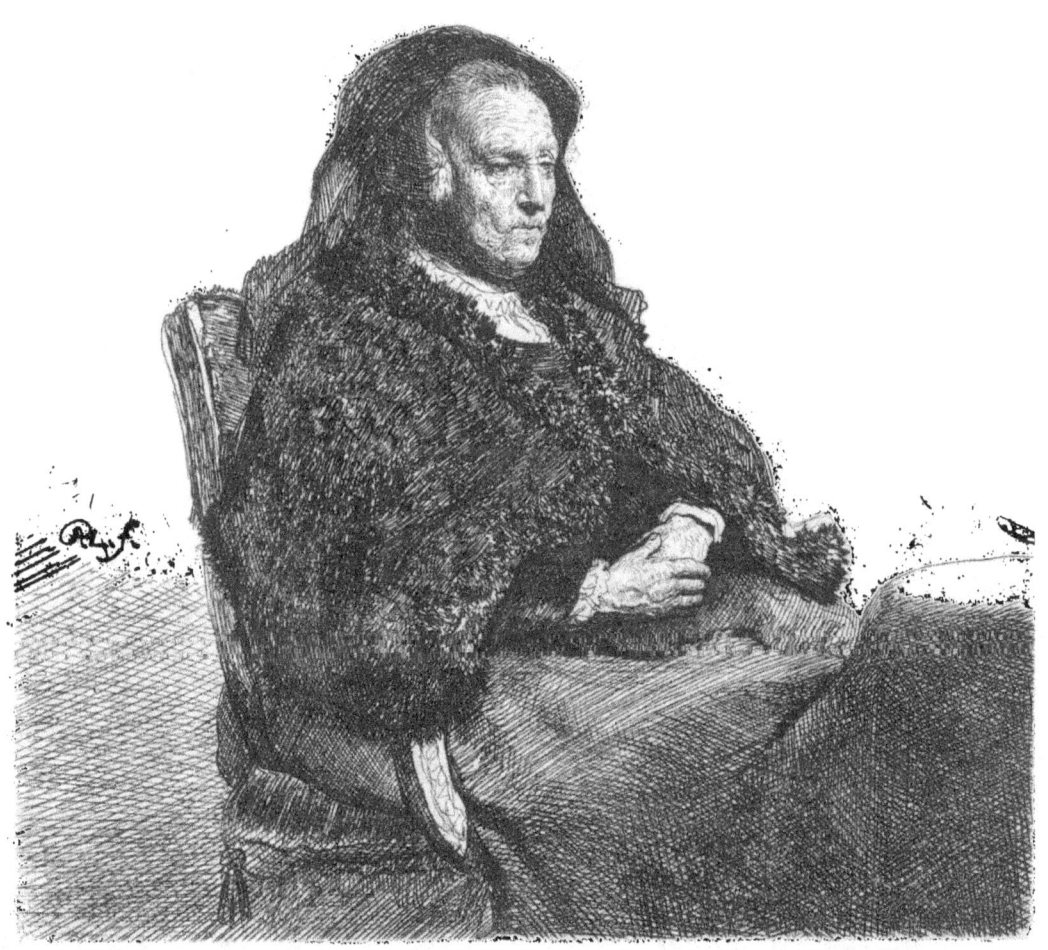

invent a new. Yet, in each work, he remains as faithful to the style determined upon for that work as if he had never mastered any other. Such a power of self-direction is very rare in art. All the engravings of Lucas of Leyden, of Albert Dürer, of Schongauer, are in each case technically alike. The etchings of Ruysdael, of Ostade, of Paul Potter, are, in each case, executed on the same principles. All Titian's pen-drawings are technically the same, all Turner's etchings, if we do not consider the subject, are but one etching. Samuel Palmer laboriously brought one kind of etching to its own perfection. Tenniel's variety as a draughts-man is in subject, not in execution. Gérôme has a fixed and uniform style with the hard pencil point, the modern substitute for silver-point. Sir Frederick Leighton always draws in the same manner with black and white chalk on brown paper. All these artists, by fidelity to one method, reached and maintained a particular kind of skill, but Rembrandt had not this special practice in his favour.

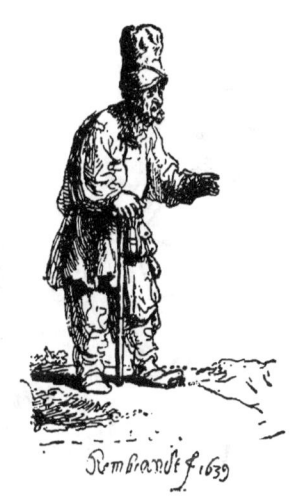

A Jew with a High Cap.
B. 133. M. 140.

For the same reason, no critic who has a special doctrine about the practice of etching can appeal to Rembrandt as an authority. When Mr. Haden says that an etching ought to be executed in one sitting to preserve the freshness of the impression we are at liberty to reply that this can be done in a small linear etching when drawing is preserved but light and shade only indicated, as, for example, in the little plate of *A Jew with a High Cap* (B. 133. M. 140.), or that it can be done in a larger plate when all accuracy of drawing is abandoned as in *The Large Lion Hunt* (B. 114. M. 272.), but that all etchings by Rembrandt in which drawing and any approach to complete shading are united must of necessity have occupied several sittings and certainly did so. If, on the other hand, a critic were to maintain with Samuel Palmer that so long as labour is intelligent the value of a work of art is increased in exact proportion with the amount of toil bestowed upon it we might answer that there are many plates by Rembrandt, very slightly executed, such, for example, as *The Bull* (B. 253. M. 289.), or the little *Resurrection of Lazarus* (B. 72. M. 215), to which nothing could have been added even by the master himself without destruction as they are already complete according to the style of execution adopted. To turn a sketch into what is called a finished drawing is to destroy the sketch and substitute

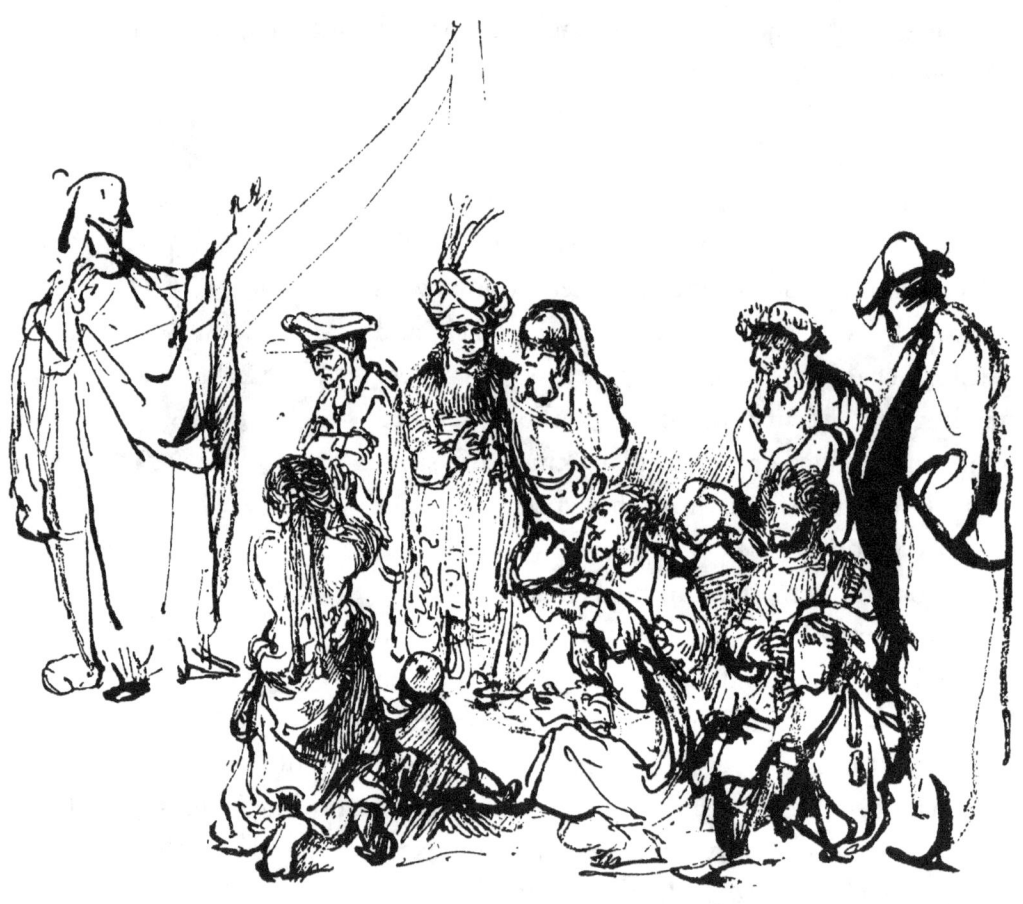

A Sketch for the Hundred Guilder Print.

another thing in its place. There is of course, no objection to finishing a thing in its own sense. We have a beautiful unfinished etching by Rembrandt, *An Old Man lifting his Hand to his Cap* (B. 259. M. 139.), in which the head, hand, and cap are carried as far as the etcher intended, the rest being indicated, apparently for future work. To complete such an etching would be to respect the work already done and go on elsewhere in harmony with it.

There is another doctrine professed and acted upon by some modern etchers (I know one who is quite faithful to it) that all work in original etching ought to be executed directly from nature. We have reasons for believing that Rembrandt did occasionally work from nature on the copper. The story is that once at Six's country house, where Rembrandt was present at an early dinner, there was no mustard. The host sent to fetch some from the village, and Rembrandt betted that before the servant (who was a slow fellow) returned he would etch a plate. He accordingly drew on copper the subject thereby immortalised as *Six's Bridge* (B. 208. M. 313.), which was visible through the window. If this story (told by Gersaint) is true, as it well may be, it shows that Rembrandt had a prepared plate with him, ready to do a landscape directly from nature, and it is highly probable that *The Goldweigher's Field* (B. 234. M. 326.) and several other plates that might be mentioned were done in the same way, though not so rapidly.[1] On the other hand, we have good evidence that some of the most important plates were done either from complete drawings of the whole subject or from experimental sketches of their different parts. I have not space to mention all the plates belonging to one or the other of these two categories, but amongst the important and most celebrated works I may mention *The Death of the Virgin* and *Christ Healing the Sick* (the Hundred Guilder Print) as executed with the help of preparatory studies of parts, which are well known to us, whilst as to portraits we have in the British Museum the original drawing of *Cornelis Anslo*, from which the etching was made. The etching of *Joseph telling his Dreams* (B. 37. M. 205.) is also an example of etching prepared for by previous work, as Rembrandt had made first a *grisaille* of the whole subject and afterwards a red chalk drawing of the figure of Jacob. Every kind of etching, even including the elaborate kind of tone-etching which has been adopted for the interpretation of pictures, may claim authority from the various and

---

[1] I had nearly written *not in such a hurry*, but that would have been inaccurate, as Rembrandt, with the consummate power of self-direction that we have been noticing, merely decided to adopt his most summary means of expression, and then hurried himself no more than the slow Dutchman who had gone to fetch the mustard.

versatile practice of the great master. If any one asserts that linear expression is a legitimate purpose in etching he certainly has Rembrandt on his side, but if he says that it is the only legitimate purpose of the art, then Rembrandt answers with tone plates like his *St. Jerome; in the dark manner* (B. 105. M. 214.), or he combines the most vigorous, and I may say magical, use of line with powerful and massive shading as in *The Presentation; in Rembrandt's dark manner* (B. 50. M. 243.).

III

I have still to consider the question of the spurious plates, and that of assistance given to Rembrandt by pupils or other artists in plates that were designed by him and probably more or less worked upon by his own hand. I was prepared to go into these questions fully, but limits of space and time compel me to be laconic, so that I can only give results. This can be done most quickly by a list with a few words of commentary.

The Descent from the Cross (B. 81. M. 187.). The large etching of this subject. Rembrandt himself first etched it on the same scale and with elaborate shading, all by his own hand. The etching ground, having been badly composed or ill-applied, did not resist the acid so that the plate was ruined beyond redemption in the biting. Three proofs were taken and the plate abandoned, but a second etching was made from it, a copy in which the drawing is vulgar and the shading commonplace, but the biting clear and sound. The copy is obviously not by Rembrandt himself, though made under his supervision. It is a commercial plate.

Ecce Homo (B. 77. M. 200.). Also a large commercial plate done by some assistant under Rembrandt's supervision, the etcher proceeding as a copyist (we know this from proofs of the work in progress) and guided by Rembrandt's corrections, but, of course, unable to give Rembrandt's handling in the shaded parts whilst he vulgarised his drawing. What remains of the original author is the composition, and the general arrangement of chiaroscuro.

The Raising of Lazarus (B. 73. M. 188.). Here the share of Rembrandt himself is rather more difficult to determine. Judging from his usual habits I should say that he would never have been at the trouble to shade the arched border in this way. Several plates by Rembrandt are arched, but in a sketchy manner. If, then, an assistant was employed for the border he probably did other work besides, most likely all the heavy shading, perhaps all the figure or Christ and the figures to the left. Lazarus and the astonished spectators to the right are drawn without useless labour and display great power of expression, but if the reader will compare the manual execution with the firm, clear, and decided drawing of the faces in *The Hundred Guilder Print* he will see that these, though cleverly executed, do not display the same marvellous use of line. Mr. Haden thinks that the arrangement of the subject and the "melodramatic action" are not like Rembrandt. We know, indeed, the small *Resurrection of Lazarus* (B. 72. M. 215.), which is remarkable for the absence of stage effect. My own conclusion is that the framework and all the heavy shading are certainly not Rembrandt's handiwork, whilst Lazarus and the spectators near him are very doubtful.

The Good Samaritan (B. 90. M. 185.). A laborious commercial plate, very different from the preceding. After the sublime we come down to the pretty. What strikes me in this plate is that it belongs strictly to its own time. Its interpretation of nature and its peculiar finish are of the seventeenth century, all through, but Rembrandt's work in etching distinguishes itself from modern work by sheer superiority, not by being old-fashioned. The invention of the subject has been traced by Vosmaer to J. van de Velde. Mr. Haden attributes the execution to Ferdinand Bol.

The Mountebank or Charlatan (B. 129. M. 117.). Mr. Haden refers to Vosmaer as having attributed the design of *The Charlatan* to J. van de Velde, but Vosmaer only mentions the *Charlatan* in a list of things of a certain date and his remark did not refer to this etching but to *The Pancake Woman*.[1] This little plate is of first-rate excellence, and Rembrandt's.

---

[1] Vosmaer is giving a list of etchings executed at a certain time, and mentions, amongst others, "*le Charlatan, la Faiseuse de Galettes*—pièce qui rappelle beaucoup une estampe de J. Van de Velde." The reader sees that the word *pièce*, which is in the singular number, refers to one etching only, and that the last mentioned.

The Pancake Woman (B. 124. M. 264.). Mr. Haden says that J. Van de Velde is "the reputed author" of *The Pancake Woman*, and refers to Vosmaer as an authority, but Vosmaer did not attribute either the design or the execution to Van de Velde, he merely said that the etching reminded him very much of a print by that artist. I have always been struck by something foreign to Rembrandt's genius in the scheme of this very cleverly executed plate. He may have accepted a suggestion.

Three Oriental Heads. First Head, Full Face, "Jacob Cats" (B. 286. M. 122.), *Second Head, a Profile to the Left* (B. 287. M. 123.), *Third Head, a Profile to the Right* (B. 288. M. 124.).

There is nothing by Rembrandt resembling these heads either in conception or execution, and there are two plates by Lievens resembling them in subject and treatment but less bitten. Mr. Haden believes all three to be by Lievens, who had a taste for staring eyes and heavy head-dresses. To this M. Emile Michel replies that Lievens never was a pupil of Rembrandt, and it seems that he lived away from him. As there is a certain lightness of hand in Lievens that there is not here, and as the conception is obviously influenced by Lievens, I should conclude that the plates were done by some contemporary unknown to us.

A Beggar and a Companion Piece (B. 177. M. 112.). Easily recognisable by the inscriptions *t'is vinnich Kout* and *dats niet.*

Suggested by two plates of Beham with inscriptions identical in sense though not verbally the same. These with Rembrandt's name are cleverly executed but not so delicately as many of his beggars. Mr. Haden thinks that Savry etched them. Vosmaer mentions a sketch by Rembrandt with the first inscription. He may have made two sketches, etched afterwards, somewhat heavily, by another hand, under his direction or by his leave.

St. Jerome sitting at the Foot of a Tree (B. 100. M. 190.). I give Mr. Middleton's title. Mr. Haden calls the plate "St. Jerome in Meditation," which may easily confuse the reader, as Charles Blanc calls his 76 (M. 210.), *St. Jérôme en Méditation* (*manière noire*) and his 77 (M. 176.), *St. Jérôme en Méditation* (*Vieillard Homme de Lettres*).

Mr. Haden says that this little plate, easily known by the curious heraldic lion (the size of a greyhound), is by Bol. Though effective in its own way as an arrangement of lights and darks, and prettily executed in a neat old-fashioned style we may be sure that it was neither designed nor executed by Rembrandt.

The Flight into Egypt; a small upright Print (B. 52. M. 184.). I have no belief in the authenticity of this little etching, which would be creditable to a minor artist.

Adverse Fortune (B. 111. M. 262.). Very unlike Rembrandt, both in conception and execution.

The Gold Weigher (B. 281. M. 138). From a design by Rembrandt but mainly executed by some inferior and more mechanical hand. The head and shoulders of the principal figure are believed to be by Rembrandt himself.

Rembrandt drawing from a Model (B. 192. M. 284.). Probably sketched by the master to be shaded by some assistant, and then abandoned before the shading was finished.

St. Jerome, an unfinished Piece (B. 104. M. 234.). Mr. Haden says that this is from a drawing by Titian sold in London at Dr. Wellesley's sale which was still recent in 1877. The lion, however, was absent from the drawing and the saint's place was occupied by a recumbent figure of Venus.

Mr. Haden does not say that the drawing has been reversed in the etching, so we may infer that it was not. It was Titian's habit in work that he did not correct with the square always to incline lines to the right. We find an inclination in the same direction here (see buildings). Rembrandt himself had not this tendency.

The landscape has been executed cleverly on a principle not usually Rembrandt's, objects presenting themselves in the flat as if cut out of card-board (see tree trunk). It reminds one of Félix Buhot's style with flat facets and short, decided strokes, a manually skilful style, but unlike Rembrandt's most personal way of etching. The figure of the saint may be by him.

Jan Antonides van der Linden (B. 264. M. 167.). Charles Blanc thought that changes made after the fourth state of this portrait were modern. M. Dutuit thinks that changes after the third state are not Rembrandt's. Mr. Middleton agrees, in substance, with M. Dutuit. In other words the greater part of the shading has been added by somebody else.

To me the whole plate is unsatisfactory, considered as a Rembrandt. The face may be creditable and has some quiet character, but anybody could etch the costume and the background, and as for the hand it is wooden and the forefinger a mere stick. It is very inferior to Rembrandt's usual incisive marking of character in hands.

The Onion Woman (B. 134. M. 66.). Mr. Middleton attributes the coarse and ugly appearance of this plate to over-biting, but over-biting would not affect the original intelligence of treatment in the use of line which is here mediocre and destitute of Rembrandt's usual delicacy of observation. Mr. Middleton argues that the execution here is no worse than that of *Lazarus Klap* (B. 171. M. 72.). Perhaps both plates may have been executed by Rembrandt in a lazy mood. " It is impossible," says Mr. Ruskin, " to bring drawing to any point of fine rightness with half-applied energy."

The Little Dog Sleeping (B. 158. M. 267.). I like the little doggie who sleeps soundly and who for the last two centuries has been sleeping more soundly still. Rembrandt, who took an interest in sleep, may have been tempted by the subject. Mr. Middleton says, " It is an open question whether *The Little Dog Sleeping* is the work of Rembrandt at all." A copy is in existence in which the sharp linear touches are wanting. The best plate is still inferior to *The Hog* (B. 157. M. 227.) and even to the *Sketch of a Dog* (B. 371. M. 266.) in the use of line, but it is well lighted and was admitted as authentic in the Burlington Club exhibition of 1877.

Besides the plates already given in this list there are a number of landscapes, principally of small size, what may be called pocket plates, that have been unwarrantably attributed to Rembrandt, and others that are doubtful. One of the best of these is a dry-point *Landscape, with a Fisherman in a Boat* (B. 243. M. rej. 19.), which previous catalogue makers had accepted, but which Mr. Middleton rejects. The difficulty in ascribing it to Rembrandt lies in the fact that we have no other dry-point certainly by him, of a similar subject, with which to compare it, and bitten plates do not afford materials for a technical comparison. The execution here is simple and modern-looking, but the distance is not so refined in treatment as many of Rembrandt's distances. I have no hesitation in rejecting the unmeaning scrawl called *Landscape, with a Canal and a Man*

Fishing (B. 244. M. rej. 8.), though an impression of it has been sold for the relatively prodigious sum of £148. There may be twenty minutes' work in this perfectly worthless performance. I agree, too, with the rejection of *A Landscape with five Cottages, unfinished* (B. 255. M. rej. 12.). The subject might have interested Rembrandt, but the execution is much weaker and less assured than his. There is a long-shaped *Land-*

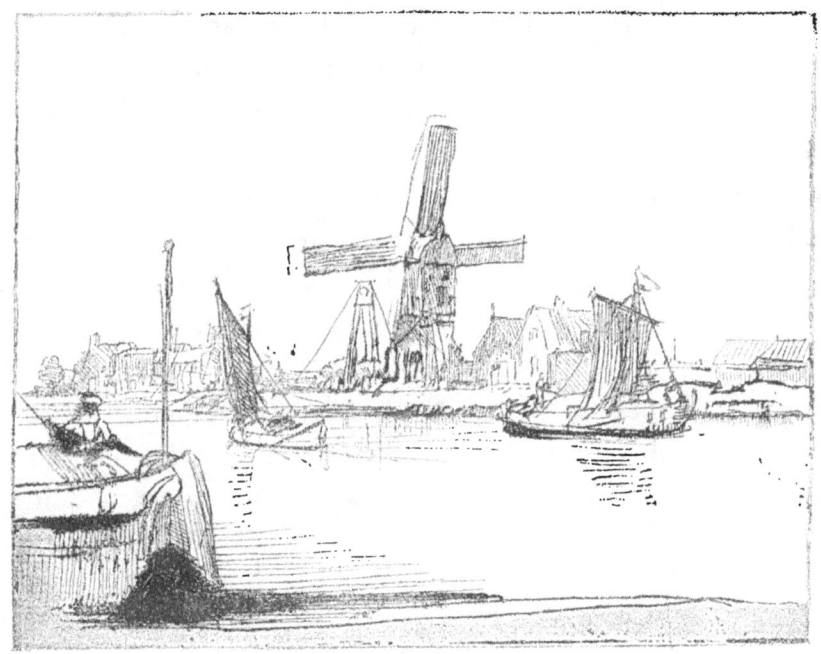

Landscape with a Fisherman in a Boat. B. 243. M. rej. 19.

scape, with a clump of Trees by the Road Side (B. 229. M. rej. 15.), which admirably expresses the peculiar character of Dutch scenery, with the road on a dyke above the level of the polders, but the workmanship is certainly not Rembrandt's.

I have not space to go through all the rejected landscapes, and have already invited the reader to the study of some undoubtedly authentic ones, by which he will be able to form his own judgment.

It is much easier to say that Rembrandt did not execute certain pieces of work than to affirm who did execute them, and it is safer to accept the negative part of Mr. Haden's criticism than the positive. For example, it appears certain now that Lievens and van Vliet were never pupils of Rembrandt, and in 1631 Lievens had left Holland. There may have been a difficulty about Bol's collaboration on account of his age, as he was only sixteen in 1632. Besides, it is always difficult to *name* assistants, especially when their work is mixed up with that of the master. There is a celebrated and successful living etcher from pictures who has often employed an assistant whom I know personally. I am familiar with the styles of both artists, but should not be able to separate their work on the same plate. The collaboration is kept secret and not a critic or other artist living has ever suspected it, still less has he been able to guess the assistant's name. I know it because he told me.

Just a word in conclusion. I have been studying the works of Rembrandt's immediate predecessors and contemporaries in etching with a view to understand his relative position more accurately. The result has been only to deepen my sense of the master's incomparable greatness, of his sterling originality, and especially of that wonderful quality in him by which he does not belong to the seventeenth century but quite as much to the closing years of the nineteenth. In like manner, when it comes, he will be at home in the twentieth century, and in many another after it.

INDEX

www.ingramcontent.com/pod-product-compliance
Lightning Source LLC
Chambersburg PA
CBHW081301170526
45165CB00011B/3373